# 101 LEADER-SHIP INSIGHTS

## Bob Phillips and Del Walinga

HARVEST HOUSE PUBLISHERS
EUGENE, OREGON

Cover design by Kyler Dougherty

For bulk, special sales, or ministry purchases, please call 1-800-547-8979.
Email: Customerservice@hhpbooks.com

**101 Leadership Insights**
Copyright © 2021 by Bob Phillips and Del Walinga
Published by Harvest House Publishers
Eugene, Oregon 97408
www.harvesthousepublishers.com

ISBN 978-0-7369-8356-3 (pbk.)
ISBN 978-0-7369-8357-0 (eBook)

Library of Congress Cataloging-in-Publication Data

Names: Phillips, Bob, author. | Walinga, Del, author.
Title: 101 leadership insights / Bob Phillips, Del Walinga.
Description: Eugene, Oregon : Harvest House Publishers, [2021] |
Identifiers: LCCN 2020054221 (print) | LCCN 2020054222 (ebook) | ISBN 9780736983563 (trade paperback) | ISBN 9780736983570 (ebook)
Subjects: LCSH: Leadership--Religious aspects--Christianity.
Classification: LCC BV4597.53.L43 P488 2021 (print) | LCC BV4597.53.L43 (ebook) | DDC 253--dc23
LC record available at https://lccn.loc.gov/2020054221
LC ebook record available at https://lccn.loc.gov/2020054222

**Printed in the United States of America**

21 22 23 24 25 26 27 28 29 / BP-RD/ 10 9 8 7 6 5 4 3 2 1

# Contents

# Personal Fulfillment—Part I

*Finding happiness and fulfillment comes about when you discover
God's plan and purpose for your life and the unique
contribution that only you can make.*

~R.E. PHILLIPS

MANY PEOPLE WORK AT JOBS THEY DISLIKE. They know they have to have employment to make a living and support their families...but they feel discouraged, disheartened, and depressed. Sometimes they simply feel bored or very unfulfilled.

Are you working at a job you *can do* and *have to do*, or are you working at a job you *want to do*? Are you getting up each day and saying, "I have to go to work." Or when you wake up do you think, "I can hardly wait to get to work"? What do you really enjoy doing? In what circumstances do you discover a feeling of competence, confidence, and usefulness?

How would you like some help in finding the right job for you? Would you like to understand the type of position that would bring you the most fulfillment and satisfaction? Would you like to have excitement and a natural energy when you go to work every day? Then read on.

A number of years ago I was exposed to a program that gives insight as to the style of work that best fitted my personality. It also helped me realize the types of jobs or positions that would steal away my enthusiasm and would lead to discomfort at work.

It was an inventory designed by Bobb Biehl called Team Profile. The profile suggests there are three basic phases to most jobs and projects. The first phase is the Design Phase, the second is the Development Phase, and the third is the Stable Phase. In between phase one and two is a combination Design/Development phase. And in between phase two and three is a combination Development/Stable phase.

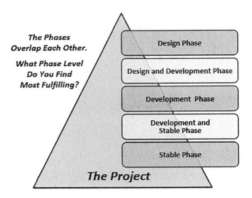

When it comes to the three main phases of most work, which one do you identify with? Do you like to be the one to come up with original ideas? Do you prefer theory and philosophy about a subject or project? Would you prefer to set goals and work on other people's ideas and polish them and improve them?

**I PREFER WORKING IN THE FOLLOWING PHASE:**

( ) Design ( ) Design/Develop ( ) Develop ( ) Develop/Stable ( ) Stable

Or would you be happy managing the idea or project after it has been designed and developed? This would include long-term goals, details, and administration of the project or task.

*No one achieves greatness by becoming a generalist.*
*You don't hone a skill by diluting your attention to its development.*
*The only way to get to the next level is focus.*

~JOHN C. MAXWELL

# Personal Fulfillment—Part II

*You are not here merely to make a living. You are here in order to
enable the world to live more amply, with greater vision, with a
finer spirit of hope and achievement. You are here to enrich the
world, and you impoverish yourself if you forget the errand.*

~WOODROW WILSON

IN THE PREVIOUS ARTICLE, WE LOOKED at the three main
phases—Design, Develop, and Stable—with two in-between phases.
Now we would like to consider characteristics of the people who work
in each of these five phases.

**DESIGNERS**—enjoy coming up with original ideas, concepts, and
models. They like to talk about theory, philosophy, and various views. If
problems are solved, or if they get bored, they like to move on to something new. Their focus can range from a few hours to a few months.

**DESIGNER/DEVELOPERS**—also like to come up with original
ideas. Their strong contribution is to make original ideas practical and
functioning. Their desire is to pass the project or task on to someone
else...so they can begin a new and exciting challenge.

**DEVELOPERS**—enjoy taking other people's ideas and concepts
and expanding on them. They have a special skill in polishing, enhanc-
ing, developing, and getting projects off the ground. Their focus for a
project often ranges from six months to two years. After this much time,
they desire to pass the project on to more detailed individuals. They are
goal oriented and are great launchers.

**DEVELOPER/STABLIZERS**—like to refine ideas, programs, and
processes even further and are happy about taking on assignments that
run from two to five years. They prefer to work on one project at a time.
Often they like to become a specialist and improve outcomes. They like

to focus on results, maximizing performance, and attention to cost effectiveness. If problems occur, they are the ones that other team members look to for solutions.

**STABLIZERS**—are control, efficiency, and technique specialists. They keep the organization and all of the details running smoothly. They are highly predictable and enjoy routine. They can easily keep focused and work on projects for five to twenty-five years. They are safety and risk conscious and like to *ensure* quality in all areas. Change is something they find a little disconcerting and difficult.

| Designer | Designer Developer | Developer | Developer Stabilizer | Stabilizer |
|---|---|---|---|---|

| | |
|---|---|
| *Designer* | One who Most Enjoys exploring theoretical essence with lesser interest in immediate practical application |
| *Designer Developer* | One who Most Enjoys the process of influencing people by making their own original ideas become practical the first time |
| *Developer* | One who Most Enjoys the challenge of implementing someone else's outstanding idea—that has worked at least once |
| *Developer Stabilizer* | One who Most Enjoys "refining" and improving ideas of others and maximizing results |
| *Stabilizer* | One who Most Enjoys controlling, maintaining, improving, and expanding existing programs |

*For further information on the Team Profile go to BobbBiehl.com.*

**I SEE MYSELF AS MORE OF
THE FOLLOWING PERSONALITY:**

( ) Designer ( ) Design/Developer ( ) Developer
( ) Developer/Stabilizer ( ) Stabilizer

*Choose a career you love, give it the best there is in you,
seize your opportunities, and be a member of the team.*

~BENJAMIN FRANKLIN FAIRLESS

# Identifying as a Leader

*Become the kind of leader that people would follow*
*voluntarily even if you had no title or position.*

~BRIAN TRACY

HOW DO OTHER PEOPLE RESPOND TO YOUR LEADER-SHIP? Do you sense they follow your direction without question, or do you pick up some hesitation? In other words, do the people you oversee affirm your leadership by following you?

Taking on the role of a leader requires guiding and inspiring others. How are you doing in this area? Are you impacting your organization with time-tested leadership skills? Are you providing a positive example to follow in your own home and at work? In short, are you giving others a living example of someone they would like to follow?

In general, good leaders do not blame fate for their failures, nor luck for their successes. Good leaders accept responsibility for their lives, as well as the lives of those who are under their direct sphere of influence. Good leaders know that any goal worth setting is only as worthy as the effort required to achieve it. Good leaders are people like you who desire to build strong families, improve communities, and make the world a better place to live.

In his book *The Future of Leadership*, Warren Bennis suggests: "Leadership is everyone's business. Leadership is an observable, learnable, set of practices. Positions of leadership do not wait, in fact cannot wait. Leadership development starts with action."

What level of achievement and commitment are you taking to establish yourself as a leader? How are you identifying with leadership skills, leadership character traits, and leadership actions?

In the book of Exodus, Moses identified himself as a reluctant leader.

He had run away from his failure as a leader when he killed an Egyptian. He didn't think people would listen to him because he was a poor speaker. He was hesitant to confront Pharaoh. Are you dealing with reluctance in your leadership?

Remember, God told Moses that He would help him, He would be with him, and He would give him strength to carry out his leadership role. The same God who helped Moses will help you.

Author Simon Sinek reminds us, "A boss has the title; a leader has the people." If we have no followers, the quality of our leadership needs attention. A good way to help others identify with you as a leader includes applying the following responsibilities and actions. Ask yourself these two foundational questions as you do: Who am I? What do I want to achieve?

- Keep learning new things and share what you have learned with others.
- Commit to deadlines; keep appointments, end meetings on time.
- Recognize and accept others' opinions and ideas when appropriate.
- Become a better listener and encourager.
- Inspire others as part of a "we" team rather than "I" alone.

### Interesting Fact

Leadership is both an area of research as well as an area of practical skill and personal development. Learning about styles and concepts of leadership is important, but working to develop your individual skills in order to be recognized as a leader is crucial.

*We will not all develop to be the same kind of leader at the same pace. Leadership takes motivation, discipline, and practice. What are you waiting for?*

# Leading Yourself First

*There is nothing noble in being superior to your fellow man,
the nobility is being superior to your former self.*

~Ernest Hemingway

THE IMPORTANCE OF SELF DEVELOPMENT as both a
leader and follower cannot be overstated. As Robin Sharma suggests,
"Investing in yourself is the best investment you will ever make. It will
not only improve your life; it will improve the lives of those around you."

A lot of time is spent investing in those things that remind us just
how short life really is. Some are extremely important: family relationships, job security, and church fellowship. Others are not nearly as significant: social media, television, and computer games. What we expect
from others we must demonstrate.

Self-development has been referred to as "human capital." I prefer
to think of it as the "stewardship of life." It's a lifelong process, requiring
effort, energy, and commitment. It comes from well-developed beliefs,
values, and the skills required to succeed as a leader. Followers want and
need leaders who are positive role models.

This is no light responsibility. Actually, leaders have no choice in the
matter. No aspect of leadership is more important. When you develop as
a leader, it inspires trust from your followers. They want to follow someone who is confident, competent, and caring. Being a personal example affects others more than instruction alone. Why would followers be
motivated to follow someone they don't trust, respect, or admire?

*A leader's motivation for self-development is greatly influenced
by their personal values.*

Here are nine key competencies consistently valued by leaders and followers alike:

*Ethics*—in verbal orders and policies

*Communication*—to direct and influence

*Proficiency*—through self-study and experiences

*Decisions*—to make choices and solve problems

*Supervision*—to coordinate and evaluate

*Planning*—to organize and budget

*Developing others*—in order to build esprit de corps and confidence

*Resourcefulness*—to demonstrate skills and manage information

*Mentoring*—to overcome problems and increase knowledge

How are you doing in these nine areas? Do you need to spend some time reinforcing any of them? Leaders continue to learn and improve through self-development so they can be better servants. Selfless service requires resisting the temptation to put selfish gain, personal advantage, and self-interests ahead of what is best for the individual and the organization.

- Reflect on what needs to improve. Be honest.

- Read about what you want to improve. Is it a personal trait or skill?

- Identify others who can encourage you and role models to be patterned after.

- Create a program for personal growth. Habits produce results.

*What is used develops, and what is left unused*
*atrophies or wastes away.*

### Points to Ponder

Given all the resources to develop self,
what changes would you make?

Could you suppress potential bad behavior and
opt for the potential for good behavior?

*Every moment of one's existence, one is growing*
*into more or retreating into less.*

~ NORMAN MAILER

*Personal development is a major time saver. The better you become,*
*the less time it takes to achieve your goals.*

~ BRIAN TRACY

# Influence

*If your actions inspire others to dream more, learn more,*
*do more, and become more, you are a leader.*

-John Quincy Adams

LEADERSHIP HAS SIMPLY BEEN DEFINED by one word: *influence*. It has been said that at least ten people watch everyone's behavior. When you serve as a leader, you influence far more than ten people. Whether or not you like it, you're in the spotlight. People are watching what you say and do. Influence involves inspiration. Influence can encourage. Influence has the ability to give guidance.

Now, for the kicker: A leader's influence can be both positive and negative. For example, a certain kind of "leader" can inspire gang members to rob and murder. A certain kind of "leader" can inspire deceptiveness, prejudice, and greed. All leadership offers guidance and has a definite impact. However, misused influence can bring about catastrophic results. Just turn on the news and see the negative influence of riots.

A leader who exerts positive influence is a leader who guides others in the right direction and imparts positive traits, habits, and actions. This helps to create positive attitudes. Positive influence is an incentive toward excellence in both the individual, the overall culture of your organization, your family, and the nation.

How are you doing as a leader and companion of others? Your words and behavior are on view for everyone to see.

*Do not be so deceived and misled!*
*Evil companionships, (communion, associations)*
*corrupt and deprave good manners and morals and character.*

1 Corinthians 15:33 AMPC

As author Ken Blanchard stated, "The key to successful leadership today is influence, not authority." Harry A. Overstreet suggests, "The very essence of all power to influence lies in getting the other person to participate." All of us need to be encouraged to work on our skills of influencing others in a positive manner. People admire leaders who have helped them stretch and receive recognition. Here are some steps to consider:

Show you are a trusted leader. Ask others, "What can I do for you?"

Build positive relationships. Tell others, "I believe in you."

Connect with people. Invest your time with a one-on-one lunch.

Extend honor. Invite others to share their ideas.

Create opportunities. Allow others to master small challenges.

### Consider This

Leadership alone provides a limited source of persuasion. Successful leaders recognize that in order to be effective, they cannot rely solely on directives, tactics, or coercion.

*Influence others in such a way that it builds them up, encourages, and edifies them so they in turn can duplicate it with others.*

# Change and Transition

*The measure of intelligence is the ability to change.*

~Albert Einstein

"CHANGE THE LEADER, CHANGE THE ORGANIZATION" is often viewed and stated as the key to making any successful difference. Yet, resistance to change is universal. The idea of introducing and accepting change is a difficult task, as well as a heavy responsibility.

How many leaders does it take to change a lightbulb? Zero! Nobody likes change. Charlie Brown asks Linus, "What would you do if you felt no one liked you?" Linus replies, "Well, I'd try to look at myself objectively to see what I could do to improve." "I don't like that answer," says Charlie Brown. We smile. But we have all been there. The only one who likes a change is the newborn baby.

Moving from who we are as leaders to who we desire to be as leaders will involve change. Taking a new business or new idea from the known to the unknown will involve change. Whether it's our personal attitude and motivation for change, or if it is a new technology and technical skill required for change, there is difficulty in navigating previously inexperienced territory.

Change creates opportunity for growth along with the potential for loss. A new job, a new boss, and a new assignment could be either good or bad. Adjusting to retirement, a relocation, or a new church can be easy or hard. Within these circumstances, change is situational. It's goal oriented. What lies between the "old" and the "new" is an unknown reality. This adjustment to change is the transition needed to complete the change process. It's letting go. It's an internal process. It's a reorientation and a coming to terms with what is taking place. Whether unpredictable, reactive, planned, anticipatory, incremental, or all at once, change is always inevitable. The key is that all change requires leadership. Leaders recognize that change, personally and organizationally, comes through a process of accurate information, overcoming objections, and an objective look at the effect on individual needs.

A quote by Martin Luther King Jr. sums up for us a healthy view of change, both organizationally and personally:

> *We ain't what we oughta be.*
> *We ain't what we want to be.*
> *We ain't what we gonna be.*
> *But, thank God, we ain't what we was.*

In any set of circumstances, there are opposing forces that require a response. Change involves overcoming those forces that both demand and resist change. Which group, if any, are you currently finding yourself in? Which group do you think represents your organization?

### Forces Demanding Change

| | | |
|---|---|---|
| Economical | Technological | Legal |
| Political | Social | Environmental |
| Expectations of others | International | Present way is ineffective |

*These represent outside factors and influences.*
*Ignore these at risk of your own peril.*

**Forces Resisting Change**

| | | |
|---|---|---|
| Fear of failure | Tradition | Vested interests |
| Work required | Lack of skills | No perceived need |
| Negative results | Routine habits | Lack of respect for the leader |

*These represent inside opinions and beliefs*
*Ignore these at the risk of another's peril.*

### Good Rule of Thumb

View change not as something being done to us, but as something we can be a part of and control.

# Anger

*It is easy to fly into a passion—anybody can do that—but to be angry
with the right person to the right extent and at the right time
and with the right object and in the right way—that is not easy,
and it is not everyone who can do it.*

~**ARISTOTLE**

STRONG FEELINGS OF TENSION, ANNOYANCE, and displeasure cause anger to raise its ugly head. It occurs when you feel violated, or something unfair or unkind has happened. It's easy to get angry when you think someone has done you or another person wrong. Anger simply alerts you to something you perceive as important to you.

We often look at anger as a negative emotion because it has a strong tendency to disrupt and destroy relationships. There is a positive side to anger when it's directed toward injustice and corruption. We need to be angry at crime, waste, and violence.

Do you have a tendency to get angry easily? I read about one survey that suggested that women get angry about three times a week and men about six times a week. It went on to suggest that women more often get angry with other people, and men more often get angry with objects. A man might be working on a project and become frustrated because it isn't coming together like it should...so he throws a hammer against a wall. Of course, I'm sure you never get angry with people or objects.

The Bible addresses the topic of anger on more than 230 occasions. Let's take a few moments and see if we can gain any insights.

*As surely as a wind from the north brings cold,
just as surely a retort causes anger.*

~Proverbs 25:23

*As the churning of cream yields butter,*
*and a blow to the nose causes bleeding,*
*so anger causes quarrels.*

~Proverbs 30:33

*It is harder to win back the friendship of an offended brother*
*than to capture a fortified city. His anger*
*shuts you out like iron bars.*

~Proverbs 18:19

*A wise man restrains his anger and overlooks*
*insults. This is to his credit.*

~Proverbs 19:11

*If you are angry, don't sin by nursing your grudge.*
*Don't let the sun go down with you still angry—get over it quickly;*
*for when you are angry, you give a mighty foothold to the devil.*

~Ephesians 4:26-27

*Stop being mean, bad-tempered, and angry.*
*Quarreling, harsh words,*
*and dislike of others should have no place in your lives.*
*Instead, be kind to each other, tenderhearted, forgiving one another,*
*just as God has forgiven you because you belong to Christ.*

~Ephesians 4:31-32

Before you read on...stop a moment and take an honest look at anger in your life. Are you an impatient, angry, and unforgiving person? Do you wallow in past hurts and resentments? Are you carrying around a grudge and nursing it like it's something precious? Is that really working for you? Maybe it's time to stop ripping off the scabs of hurtful experiences and let God do some healing in your life. Sound good?

# People Watching

*He alone is an acute observer, who can observe
minutely without being observed.*

~JOHANN KASPAR LAVATER

W E ALL TEND TO LISTEN TO OTHER PEOPLE and watch their behavior half-heartedly. We then quickly move from casual observation to subjective evaluation and judgment. Many times our hasty judgment results in emotional turmoil, producing annoying relationships and conflict between people.

The more we become aware of the behavior of other people and ourselves, the more we will be able to control our responses. And learning to control our responses and reactions in our relationships will reduce tensions and help us get along better. King Solomon said, "A gentle answer turns away wrath, but a harsh word stirs up anger" (Proverbs 15:1 NIV). Our behavior and our reactions to the behavior of other people can positively influence our relationships.

Wouldn't it be helpful if you could tell if someone was being untruthful with you and lying about a matter? You can by observing their nonverbal behavior. Often people who are not being completely honest have the tendency to put their hand in front of their mouth while they're talking with you. And if they don't use their hand, they will sometimes put a pencil or pen over their lips while talking with you. Sometimes they will begin to cough a little while talking with you. To gain insight in reading body language, two books are recommended: *How to Read a Person Like a Book* by Nierenberg, Calero, and Grayson, and *Body Language* by Julius Fast.

*Look in the face of the person to whom you are speaking if you wish to know his
real sentiments, for he can command his words more easily than his countenance.*

~LORD CHESTERFIELD

## People Watching Application

This next week begin to sharpen your body language skills by observing two specific behaviors each day. Deliberately choose to concentrate on the actions and behaviors of your family, friends, strangers, and those you work with. Be alert to what you can learn from listening to the content of words and tone of voice and by watching nonverbal body language. You will find it an insightful exercise.

| MONDAY | |
|---|---|
| **Watch** how *People Walk* | Fast or Slow |
| **Listen** to how *People Talk* | Loud or Quiet |

| TUESDAY | |
|---|---|
| **Be aware** of the *Tone of Voice* | Happy or Sad |
| **Be alert** to the *Individual's Posture* | Rigid or Relaxed |

| WEDNESDAY | |
|---|---|
| **Focus** on *Eye Contact* | Direct or Indirect |
| **Be attentive** to *Speech Content* | Facts or Feelings |

| THURSDAY | |
|---|---|
| **Concentrate** on *Body Gestures* | Many or Few |
| **Note** people's *Reaction to Others* | Outgoing or Restrained |

| FRIDAY | |
|---|---|
| **Observe** how others *Respond Under Stress* | Anger or Fear |
| **Be mindful** of people's *Facial Expressions* | Positive or Negative |

## Interesting Fact

Gerard Nierenberg, writing in *How to Read a Person Like a Book*, shared that in over 2,000 videotaped conflict negotiations, never once was a conflict settled where anyone in attendance had their legs crossed. Settlement was reached only when all negotiators uncrossed their legs and moved toward each other.

The next time you're in heavy discussions between parties, look to see if anyone has their legs crossed—*even if their legs are only crossed at the ankles.* Make sure that you uncross your legs and place your feet on the floor. Then begin to lean toward the other parties in a friendly manner. Keep in this position and observe to see if other people begin to follow your nonverbal leading.

# Ten Thousand Hours

*If I miss practicing on the piano one day, I can tell the difference
in my playing. If I miss practicing on the piano for two days,
my friends can tell the difference. But if I miss the practice
for three days, my audience can tell the difference.*

~Jan Paderewski

N 1993, ANDERS ERICSSON REFERENCED A STUDY involv-
ing the "practicing habits of violin students" from age five to the age of
twenty. It was estimated that it took about 10,000 hours of practice for
those individuals to become elite performers.

Malcolm Gladwell, who wrote the book entitled *Outliers*, is credited with coming up with the 10,000 Hour Principle. It basically suggests that it takes 10,000 hours of "deliberate practice" to become world
class in any field.

Does that really mean if I spend 10,000 hours studying calculus,
astrophysics, or brain surgery that I'll become an expert in that field? The
answer is yes and no. Yes, if you're really interested in a particular field of
study...but no, if you're not interested.

Spending hours alone does not guarantee mastery. Just think of the
number of people who spend years going to work and are not successful millionaires.

It's also been suggested that if you read five books on any subject
that you will be on the way to becoming an expert in that subject.
That's because most people don't read even one book on that particular subject. I could start reading five books about bird-watching, but I'll
never become an expert because I don't care about bird-watching. Success, mastery, or proficiency in any field starts with passion, focus, and

dedication. If you are not passionate about a particular subject, activity, or goal, you are guaranteed of not becoming successful or professional.

The bottom line in life is this: *We do what we want to do.* For example, how long did it take you to learn good manners? If manners mean nothing to you, it's likely that you won't have them.

Let's focus on leadership. Do you want to become a success as a leader? Do you want to make a difference in the lives of other people? Do you want to make a positive contribution to your organization, family, or the community you live in? It all comes down to your desire, passion, and concern. How important is it to you to become a leader that people want to follow?

If becoming an effective leader is important to you, you will put out the effort by reading on the subject, getting counsel and advice from other leaders, and by putting leadership principles into action. We only gain and keep what we give away.

If you were to ask me how long it took me to learn good manners, my reply would be, "I'm still learning." When it comes to leadership, it's a continual process. It's not something you have after 10,000 hours of work. It's a lifetime project. We're in the "leadership pool." We need more swimmers. Do you want to jump in?

> *Learning is the essential fuel for the leader, the source of high-octane energy that keeps up the momentum by continually sparking new understanding, new ideas, and new challenges. It is absolutely indispensable under today's conditions of rapid change and complexity. Very simply, those who do not learn do not long survive as leaders.*
>
> ~WARREN BENNIS AND BURT NANUS

# Blunders, Bobbles, and Bloopers

*To err is human, but when the eraser wears out
ahead of the pencil, you're overdoing it.*

-J. JENKINS

TAKE A MOMENT AND THINK BACK about the various leaders you've worked for. Have they been perfect? I think I know the answer. With that thought in mind, may I ask, "Have you been perfect as an employee working under them?" I think I know that answer also.

Listed below is are some blunders, bobbles, and bloopers that leaders continue to make. As you review them, make a note to learn from the blunders, and do not repeat them in your leadership.

❑ **Death of the Story Pole**—Every company or organization has a "story pole" or corporate culture. Basically, it's the history of how and why the business was started. It involves the organization's original vision and mission. It recounts the struggle to grow and contribute to society and the people who made it possible. It contains the rich heritage of principles upon which the company was established. But now, everyone is too engaged with reaching for the stars. We're too busy to remember the story of what brought us to success in the first place. Besides, the ring tone on my cell phone just went off.

❑ **Personal Growth**—Once you rise to a certain level of leadership, there's no longer a need for personal growth. It's unnecessary because you're now the top dog. Everyone must understand that you have all the answers. There's no need to read any leadership books, go to leadership seminars, or sharpen my leadership skills. Besides, who has time for all that? It would interfere with my long lunches, my golf game, and my need to leave work in the late afternoon. My personal growth comes from what I want to do, not from the stupid responsibilities that I was hired for.

- ❑ **Communication Chaos**—This occurs when job descriptions are unclear, partial information or no information is shared, and rumors abound. It basically stems from natural curiosity, the need for clarification, and the strong desire to not want to be left out. Everyone wants to be in the know. This is the biggest problem in most companies. It's something that *cannot be totally eliminated* and thus has to be continually worked on. Are we having fun yet?

- ❑ **Criticism/Complaining/Condemning**—Psychologists suggest there are three reasons for criticism: 1) We are guilty of the same thing. 2) We are miserable and want to have company and people to be on our side. 3) We want to put people down in the eyes of others…which helps to indicate that we know better, and we wouldn't act the way they do, and we are all wise and knowing about everything. Pick a number and stand in line.

- ❑ **Dirty Delegation**—There are two possible courses in dirty delegation. The first is to assign to others unpleasant jobs that are our responsibility but we don't want to do them. The second is to give them the authority and responsibility for a task and then interrupt them, micromanage them, and take back authority. Don't you just love to work for a leader like that?

- ❑ **Failing to Define Goals and Expectations**—It's very difficult to move forward when you don't know where you're going. And it's unfair, frustrating, and maddening to be held responsible and accountable for something that was never shared with you. The answer: Buy a better crystal ball.

❑ **Failing to Train**—Sometimes leadership has expectations for employees in areas for which they have no knowledge or training. It's sort of like expecting fish to climb trees. You do remember how to spell *assume* don't you?

# Conviction

*Societies are renewed—if they are renewed at all—*
*by people who believe something, care about*
*something, and stand for something.*

~JOHN GARDNER

WHEN YOU TAKE ON THE ROLE OF LEADER, it sets you apart from followers. What makes the leader different? One of the factors is conviction as opposed to uncertainty. Who wants to follow someone who is uncertain, cannot make up their mind, and is fearful about the direction the group should go? Convictions are strong and firmly held beliefs, opinions, or persuasions. Preferences are changeable; whereas, convictions are firm and solid.

You see, if you lead with doubt, the followers will become doubtful themselves. They want to follow someone who is filled with integrity, courage, and strong belief...not someone who is wishy-washy, undecided, and hesitant.

When a leader has strong conviction, it's evident to everyone. Their tone of voice, their body language, and their speech are persuasive and convincing. Convictions give you unusual strength and determination. We can see this in one of our early American founders, Patrick Henry.

> Our brethren are already in the field! Why should we stand here idle? What is it that gentlemen wish? What would they have? Is life so dear, or peace so sweet, as to be purchased at the price of chains and slavery? Forbid it, Almighty God! I know not what course others may take; but as for me, give me liberty, or give me death!

Where does conviction come from? It comes from a clear understanding of the principles of character. It has to do with morality—our understanding of what is right and good and what is wrong and bad. It shapes who we are, what we believe, how we make decisions, and what we will stand for. It gives us the courage to listen to our conscience and stand by our convictions. It gives us the ability to resist the influence of the crowd. It puts fire in our belly.

*Convictions are the mainsprings of action, the driving powers of life. What a man lives are his convictions.*

~Francis Kelley

*Conviction is worthless unless it is converted into action.*

~Thomas Carlyle

How are you doing in the area of conviction? Can you stand for right even when it's not popular? Remember, you were not hired to be liked by people. You were hired to do a job and make decisions—and sometimes you have to stand alone.

*Right is right even if everyone is against it, and wrong is wrong even if everyone is for it.*

~William Penn

# Ten Leadership Styles—Part I

*The ultimate responsibility of a leader is to facilitate
other people's development as well as his own.*

~Fred Pryor

IF YOU HAVE WORKED FOR MORE THAN ONE BOSS, you
have surely noticed they do not all lead in the same manner. On one
end, some leaders are very loose and give little direction: "You're on your
own." On the other end, they come on strong like a dictator and create
an environment of "It's my way or the highway."

Between the two extremes are a number of common leadership
methods. Most leaders can be identified with or lean toward one of the
ten different ways of leading. As you look at the following styles, see if
you identify with one of them.

### Autocratic Leadership

One leader takes on the major responsibility and control for
decision-making and rarely considers workers'
suggestions or shares any power.

### Democratic Leadership

Provides leadership that is participative and often encourages
input from team members before making a final decision.

People often say, "I don't want to be an autocratic leader." This is
because they do not want to be viewed as a dictator. They want people
to like them and not be afraid of them. However, there will be times in
your leadership experience where you will have to make tough decisions

without the input from other people in a democratic process. You cannot be soft and fuzzy when employees steal from the company, start physical fights with other staff members, or are rude to customers.

Place a check in each box that identifies your leadership style:

| Autocratic Leader | Democratic Leader |
|---|---|
| ☐ Boss | ☐ Leader |
| ☐ Sharp voice | ☐ Friendly voice |
| ☐ Command | ☐ Invitation |
| ☐ Power | ☐ Influence |
| ☐ Pressure | ☐ Stimulation |
| ☐ Demanding cooperation | ☐ Winning cooperation |
| ☐ I tell you what you should do | ☐ I tell you what I will do |
| ☐ Imposing ideas | ☐ Selling ideas |
| ☐ Domination | ☐ Guidance |
| ☐ Criticism | ☐ Encouragement |
| ☐ Faultfinding | ☐ Recognize achievement |
| ☐ Punishing | ☐ Helping |
| ☐ I tell you | ☐ Discussion |
| ☐ I decide, you obey | ☐ I suggest, I help you decide |
| ☐ Sole responsibility of boss | ☐ Shared responsibility |

In some cultures, autocratic leadership is the custom. It's a way of life. A more democratic leadership style is becoming more popular in businesses today.

*Man's capacity for justice makes democracy possible;*
*but man's inclination to injustice makes democracy necessary.*

–Reinhold Niebuhr

# Ten Leadership Styles—Part II

*When we are no longer able to change a situation,*
*we are challenged to change ourselves.*

–Victor Frankl

TYLER HAD RECENTLY BEEN PROMOTED to a midlevel management position with the Fairfax Corporation. He began to realize he needed some help with his leadership skills. He sought out some advice from Ray Osmond, who was the vice president of Fairfax.

"Ray, I'm having some trouble trying to determine what my leadership style should be. I see some good points in each of them."

"I know what you mean, Tyler. I had that same problem a number of years ago when I was promoted. I didn't want to be a bureaucratic leader that was uptight about details. I didn't want to be a laissez-faire leader that didn't care or give direction to my followers. It was my desire to be more of a servant leader."

"That's been my struggle too," said Tyler.

"It took me a little while before I realized that even as a servant leader I had to deal with 'red tape,' piles of paperwork, and other bureaucratic details. I didn't want to be that laissez-faire leader—then I discovered that I needed to 'back off' a little and not be so hands-on with everyone under me. I needed to give them breathing room so they could learn to make decisions on their own. They needed to experience and deal with both success and failure to really grow. It was then that I realized that when you enter into a leadership position, it's not just one style alone. It's a combination of different methods, depending upon the circumstances I was facing. I needed to learn to be alert, open, and flexible to the needs of the moment."

"That's helpful."

"It was then that I began to do a little study about the various types of leadership. I began to look for the good and positive traits in the different forms of leading. I wanted to include them with my servant leadership. Along with that, I also took note of the negative sides of the different styles and tried not to do them. I'm not perfect by any means, but I'm at least more directional and purposeful as I attempt to lead others."

### Transformational Leadership

Creates an environment of intellectual stimulation and inspires staff with vision, high energy, and commitment to goals.

### Laissez-faire Leadership

Central leadership basically takes a hands-off approach and allows the group to make decisions on their own and get on with their tasks.

### Bureaucratic Leadership

Creates a highly regulated environment with little innovation or creativity from the group, coupled with a very strict adherence to rules.

### Transactional Leadership

Promotes compliance by followers to a clear chain of command and uses a rewards and punishment (carrot and stick) management style.

*The first responsibility of a leader is to define reality.*
*The last is to say thank you. In between, the leader is a servant.*

~Max DePree

# Ten Leadership Styles—Part III

*For anything worth having one must pay the price; and the price is*
*always work, patience, love, self-sacrifice—no paper currency,*
*no promises to pay, but the gold of real service.*

~JOHN BURROUGHS

I N THE 1970s ROBERT GREENLEAF WROTE AN ARTICLE
about the leader as a servant. Many credit him with coming up with the
term *servant leadership*. That might have been the first use of the term, but
it is certainly not the first and greatest illustration of servant leadership.

There is no question that the greatest example of a servant leader is
Jesus Christ. Paul the apostle addresses this concept of leadership in a letter written over 2,000 years ago. It's found in Philippians 2:3-11:

> *Don't be selfish; don't try to impress others. Be humble, thinking of*
> *others as better than yourselves. Don't look out only for your own*
> *interests, but take an interest in others, too. You must have the same*
> *attitude that Christ Jesus had. Though he was God, he did not think*
> *of equality with God as something to cling to. Instead, he gave up*
> *his divine privileges; he took the humble position of a slave and*
> *was born as a human being. When he appeared in human form, he*
> *humbled himself in obedience to God and died a criminal's death*
> *on a cross. Therefore, God elevated him to the place of highest honor*
> *and gave him the name above all other names, that at the name of*
> *Jesus every knee should bow, in heaven and on earth and under the*
> *earth, and every tongue declare that Jesus Christ is Lord, to the glory*
> *of God the Father* (NLT).

Jesus Himself clarified His leadership role when He said, "Your attitude must be like my own, for I, the Messiah, did not come to be served,
but to serve, and to give my life as a ransom for many" (Matthew 20:28).

There are some who have suggested that the concept of humility or servant leadership creates the impression of weakness and a lack of leadership. Just the opposite is true. It takes great strength to choose to be a servant rather than being forced to be a servant. Our natural human nature is for others to serve and meet our needs. Most people have a tendency to want their needs and desires met regardless of the expense to others. Just look around our society today and what is broadcast in the news. How desperately we could use servant leaders rather than the self-serving leaders in the government and businesses.

### Coach Leadership

Recognizes the strengths and weaknesses of team members and attempts to get the best out of them through encouragement to improve.

### Visionary Leadership

Envisions positive potential of how the future could be changed for good and inspires the group to move toward a goal that will benefit all.

### Pacesetter Leadership

Effective in creating high performance, fast results, and an environment of lead by example and "follow me" approach to stimulate the group.

### Servant Leadership

Promotes an "others first" mindset, which involves empathy, listening, and a commitment to personal development and team unity.

*Moreover it is required in stewards that one be found faithful.*

1 Corinthians 4:2 NKJV

# Identifying Problems

*I keep six honest serving-men*
*(They taught me all I knew);*
*Their names are What and Why and When*
*and How and Where and Who.*

~Rudyard Kipling

LEADERSHIP REQUIRES SOLVING PROBLEMS. Problems can often be complex, with various contributing factors. Peter Drucker stated his greatest strength as a consultant was "to be ignorant and ask a few questions." The above quote is from Kipling's poem "I Keep Six Honest Serving-Men." Junior high school teachers, journalism instructors, and law enforcement academies have utilized it as a way to challenge students to think through solving the challenges that will be encountered.

As a leader, *Who* could refer to employees or customers. *What* could refer to products or individual departments. *Where* could refer to facilities or direction. *When* could refer to frequency or circumstances. *Why* could refer to mission, communication, or change. And *How* could refer to the manner or condition in which something exists.

*Problems* are defined as situations, persons, or things that need attention in order to be resolved. A problem can be regarded as the difference between the actual situation and a desired situation. Once a problem has been identified, its exact nature needs to be determined.

*A problem well stated is a problem half solved.*

~ Charles Kettering

A reasonable first question involving a problem would be, "Why do I sense there is a problem?" A second thought might be, "Is the problem also perceived by others?" Jim Rohn then suggests three basic questions to ask in moving forward to solve a problem: "What could I do?" "What could I read?" and "Who could I ask?"

*Every problem contains the seeds of its own solution.*

~STANLEY ARNOLD

*If I were given one hour to save the planet,*
*I would spend fifty-five minutes defining the*
*problem and only five minutes finding the solution.*

~ALBERT EINSTEIN

*A man with fifty problems is twice as alive as a man with*
*twenty-five. If you haven't got problems, you should get down*
*on your knees and ask, "Lord, don't you trust me anymore?"*

~JOHN BAINBRIDGE

Review these four basic steps and questions to identifying and dealing with problems:

- *Is anything known?* Describe the problem or concern and any background or history.

- *List the facts.* Is there a pattern or trend? Is it a subproblem or the main problem?

- *Has anything been done?* Are there comparable responses? Is there a desired outcome?

- *Are there options?* What are the potential solutions? List advantages and disadvantages. If it is determined that there is a need for a solution and a decision is required, then it's time to act. Make a decision.

## Wisdom Concerning Problems

*When solving problems, dig at the roots, not the leaves.*

~ANTHONY J. D'ANGELO

# Experience and Influence

*As iron sharpens iron, so one person sharpens another.*

~Proverbs 27:17 niv

THE CONE OF LEARNING SUGGESTS that we tend to remember 10 percent of what we read, 20 percent of what we hear, 30 percent of what we see, and 50 percent of what we see and hear. Our level of involvement is verbal and visual. However, as leaders, we need to note that we also retain 70 percent of what we say and 90 percent of what we both say and do. Our level of involvement is active. And followers want to hear directly from and interact with their leaders.

Effectively influencing and developing others requires more than providing skills and emphasizing the importance of the task. It requires personal involvement and character. Not only with dimensions of ability and performance, but with elements of integrity, personal example, and experience. This is provided through verbal and written communication that shares real experiences and invites discussion.

Dedicated leaders role model the performance to be exhibited and provide needed motivation and inspiration for followers to learn. As professor Austin Barber has noted, "All of us must speak to the hearts and souls of our students with genuine compassion. We should unselfishly give of ourselves to those whose lives and careers rest on us." It's the leader's responsibility to assist followers when necessary.

Important characteristics of a leader with positive influence include: developing personal confidence and abilities, rejecting uncontrollable emotions such as the fear of failure and rejection of others, and having a conscious awareness and coordination of what they are saying and doing while in front of others. A leader controls posture, makes eye contact, controls their voice, uses words clearly, and above all, knows the subject.

Successful leaders recognize certain principles to enhance learning. They are applicable to all leaders and followers who desire to be an influence.

*The First Step:* Attain attention and interest. This "introduction" phase is designed to focus interest on the lesson to be shared and learned. Leaders provide the motive and desire for learning. This involves arousing the recipient's curiosity and attention. It's the leader's responsibility to emphasize the importance of the topic, stress performance objective outcomes, and seek feedback and questions.

*The Second Step:* Impart the knowledge or skills to be possessed and needed. The leader's challenge is to "present" the instruction in an effective order, placing emphasis on the most critical aspects through teaching aids, demonstration, and testimonies. Imparting knowledge from personal experience includes identifying any failures and hurdles overcome in the process.

*The Third Step:* Afford the person or group the opportunity to use the information. This "application" step allows the person to actively participate and use the information gained. It should reveal the learner's grasp of details and the ability to advance. Active participation is essential.

*The Fourth Step:* Evaluate the individual or group and their ability to succeed. This "testing" phase is geared toward accountability. Followers must realize the extent of success, as well as the results of failure. The process of oral, written, or performance evaluations can serve as an indication that both effective teaching and accurate learning has occurred.

An effective leader, using experience and influence, is enthusiastic, well versed in the subject, and prepared and organized. Such leaders are goal oriented, supportive of the needs of others, and use repetitive methods. And influential leaders are open to questions and critiques. When conditions are favorable to learning, followers are in a state of readiness. Followers will desire to continue to learn due to a sense of satisfaction through their success. And followers tend to repeat experiences that are satisfying, thus building good habit patterns.

*I cannot teach anybody anything, I can only make them think.*

–Socrates

# Beliefs and Values

*Man's most valuable trait is a judicious sense of what not to believe.*

~EURIPIDES

IN STATING, "WE LEAD OUT OF OUR BELIEFS," Dr. Myles Monroe is reinforcing the fact that what leaders genuinely believe and value directly affects their lives and leadership.

Core beliefs and values are a combination of what we have experienced through seeing, hearing, and reading. It's what we spend our time thinking about. Beliefs are those ideals in which we place our confidence, trust, and hope. It is the base of our convictions.

Consider this partial list of beliefs: God, creation, democracy, life, the Constitution, faith, culture, and foundational principles. They represent our declarations about the world around us that we hold to be true. They represent our personal judgments upon which we make decisions and conclusions.

Values are those people, objects, and actions we hold of high importance, worth, and usefulness. They represent those things we desire to seek for others and ourselves. Consider this partial list of values: freedom, equality, justice, education, health, family, career, and character.

Beliefs and values can differ from person to person. Beliefs and values are internalized, forming our attitudes and opinions. Beliefs and values inspire our actions. How we communicate and demonstrate our beliefs and values reveals what we as leaders stand for. For example, if we say one of our beliefs is in the sanctity of life and that we value equality, but we are seen as sexist or racist, people would question those beliefs and values. A leader's image and reputation are affirmed by the core beliefs and values they choose to identify with.

*Try not to become a man of success but rather
try to become a man of value.*

–ALBERT EINSTEIN

Great leaders must have specific core values they adhere to—values
that others can identify with and even adopt personally. Here is a partial
list of the benefits for taking time to identify, and even articulate, your
core beliefs and values:

Promotes loyalty                              Motivates strong work ethic

Affirms relationships                         Builds team unity and morale

Cultivates healthy pride                      Enhances personal effectiveness

Inspires ethical behavior                     Gives understanding to

Develops goal consensus                       expectations

Reduces tension and stress

Leaders who take time to list their beliefs and values indicate feeling
more grounded. It helps them to stay mentally focused on their overall
leadership responsibilities. Take time to identify your top five beliefs and
values. Start by asking a basic question for each. What are those strong
influences in life that cause me to respond when they are violated? If it
helps, when identifying beliefs, think moral absolutes. When identifying values, think of those things that are invaluable.

|           Beliefs           |           Values           |
| --------------------------- | -------------------------- |
| 1._____        | 1._____       |
| 2._____        | 2._____       |
| 3._____        | 3._____       |
| 4._____        | 4._____       |
| 5._____        | 5._____       |

# Intuition

*Intuition is always right in at least two important ways;*
*It is always in response to something. It always has*
*your best interest at heart.*

~GAVIN DE BECKER

INTUITION IS THE POWER TO KNOW SOMETHING or to act a certain way without proof or evidence. Some call it instinct, a hunch, or a gut feeling. Others refer to it as a still, small inner voice that warns us of danger or exposure to physical, financial, relational, emotional, or spiritual harm. Intuition also can give us a sense of peace, comfort, and approval if we are choosing the correct decision or path to go down.

Can you recall when your intuition directed you to make a particular decision, but you ignored that inner voice? You then made a decision that was not beneficial, and you kicked yourself internally for being so stupid. I think we all have done that at some time or other.

*Trust your hunches. Hunches are usually based on facts*
*filed away just below the conscious level.*

~JOYCE BROTHERS

Where does the inner voice of intuition come from? Most likely it comes from information stored in the right and left sides of the brain—and we also cannot leave out promptings from God in our soul.

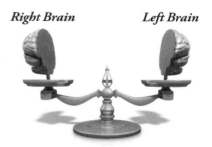

*Right Brain*          *Left Brain*

| Left Brain | Right Brain |
|---|---|
| ❑ Thinking in words | ❑ Thinking in visualization |
| ❑ Analytical | ❑ Feelings/Emotions |
| ❑ Logic | ❑ Intuition |
| ❑ Facts | ❑ Observation |
| ❑ Details | ❑ Nonverbal cues |
| ❑ Order | ❑ Imagination |
| ❑ Sequencing | ❑ Creativity |
| ❑ Linear thinking | ❑ Arts |
| ❑ Computations | ❑ Daydreaming |
| ❑ Mathematics | ❑ Optimism |

When you are confronted with a crisis, a decision, or some type of choice, intuition draws from both sides instantly. Facts and details somehow merge together with feelings and observation and create a hunch or gut feeling.

> *Whenever we need to make a very important decision it is best to trust our instincts, because reason usually tries to remove us from our dream, saying that the time is not yet right. Reason is afraid of defeat, but intuition enjoys life and its challenges.*
>
> ~Paulo Coelho

Let me illustrate intuition. Let's say you have to make an important choice between three different matters. Write down each decision (or matter) on a separate 3 x 5 card. Next, number the three cards in the order of importance, or place them in the order in which they need to be done. How did you determine the order? Why did you choose the decision you marked as number one? It was intuition that prompted you to come up with that order. Intuition always goes to the bottom line of what you really want to do. Learn to trust intuition.

> *The mind can assert anything and pretend it has proved it.*
> *My beliefs I test on my body, on my intuitional consciousness,*
> *and when I get a response there, then I accept.*
>
> ~D.H. Lawrence

# Leadership Knowledge

*Consider the questions below in relation to your leadership needs and responsibilities. Place a check in the box if it applies to you or is an area you need to work on.*

❑ **Can you organize people, tasks, and time?**

- *In my youth I stressed freedom, and in my old age I stress order. I have made the great discovery that liberty is a product of order.*—Will Durant

- *Unless a person takes charge of them, both work and free time are likely to be disappointing.*—Mihaly Csikszentmihalyi

❑ **Are you able to make decisions when information is missing?**

- *Foolish are the generals who ignore the daily intelligence from the trenches. Even then, decisions are difficult.*

❑ **Are you open to assuming responsibility for financial stewardship?**

- *Stewardship is not necessarily the things we do, but the spirit that influences the things we do.*—Wayne Clark

- *Be faithful in small things because it is in them that your strength lies.*—Mother Teresa

❑ **Can you motivate groups toward specific objectives?**

- *Lord, grant that I may always desire more than I can accomplish.*—Michelangelo

- *The world is moved by highly motivated people, by enthusiasts, by men and women who want something very much or believe very much.*—John Gardner

❑ **Do you like to plan things in which people are involved?**

    ° *I just really enjoy the process of working with other talented, creative people. There's great power in bringing diverse points of view together. It can be incredibly stimulating.*
    —Mark Parker

❑ **Do you sense when others need a helping hand?**

    ° *We're not primarily put on this earth to see through one another, but to see one another through.*—Peter De Vries

    ° *Time and money spent in helping men to do more for themselves is far better than mere giving.*—Henry Ford

❑ **Are you willing to be personally involved in counseling others?**

    ° *Without wise leadership, a nation is in trouble; but with good counselors there is safety.*—Proverbs 11:14

    ° *When you counsel someone, you should appear to be reminding him of something he had forgotten, not of the light he was unable to see.*—Baltasar Gracián

❑ **Do you get excited about the discovery of new ideas and like to share them with others?**

    ° *Ideas are like rabbits. You get a couple and learn how to handle them, and pretty soon you have a dozen.*

    ° *Great minds discuss ideas, average minds discuss events, small minds discuss people.*

❑ **Can you deal with hard facts and bad news?**

    ° *There is no man in this world without some manner of tribulation or anguish, though he be king or pope.*—Thomas à Kempis

    ° *Trouble is the thing that strong men grow by. Met the right way, it is a sure-fire means of putting iron into the victim's will and making him a tougher man.*—H. Bertram Lewis

# Criticism

*Don't be distracted by criticism. Remember, the only taste of success some people have is when they take a bite out of you.*

~ZIG ZIGLAR

HAVE YOU EVER BEEN CRITICIZED? If you haven't, cheer up! You will be someday. Everyone will experience criticism at some point from his or her family, friends, teachers, bosses, fellow employees, or even from strangers.

How do you respond when being criticized? Do you get angry and say, "Same to you, buddy!" Do you feel threatened and picked upon like a martyr? Do you just become silent and afraid to respond? Is there any help for dealing with criticism, whether it is constructive and fair or destructive and unfair?

> *Don't let people's compliments go to your head,*
> *and don't let their criticism get to your heart.*

❑ Don't respond immediately. Take a deep breath, count to ten, and breathe out slowly. Try to smile and begin to listen carefully for both facts and emotions. Listen for intention or motives. Try to understand what their complaints or concerns are. Along the way, ask questions and seek clarification.

❑ Try and remember James 1:19 (NKJV), which states, "Let every man be swift to hear, slow to speak, slow to wrath." Stay calm and control your emotions. Try not to become defensive as they pour out their dissatisfactions. Don't interrupt and begin to argue, refute, correct, or attempt to clarify misunderstanding in the midst of their unloading of their complaint.

❏ Let them get it all out of their system. Before you respond, ask, "Is there anything else? Are there any other issues that you would like to share with me?" After they share any other complaints, ask again, "Is there anything else?" Keep doing this until they say, "That's it. There's nothing else." This would be a good time to play back and respond to the accusations or complaints from the confronter. "Let me see if I've heard you correctly." Then ask, "Have I accurately understood what you've shared with me?"

*A well stated issue is a problem half solved.*

❏ Be open and evaluate if there's a grain of truth to what they are saying. Don't try to make excuses. If there are legitimate issues where you're wrong, admit it and apologize for your part. The sooner you do that, the sooner you both can get on with life.

❏ Start by saying, "Thank you for the honest sharing of your thoughts and how the situation has affected you." Then begin to clarify misunderstandings or answer questions they might have. Remember, there are always two sides to every issue. The goal is to save or reconcile the relationship, if possible, not to become defensive and win an argument.

❏ Remember, not all criticisms against you will be accurate or fair. Some people have an ax to grind, and they'll never be satisfied. In those cases, when you get kicked by a donkey, just consider the source. Remember, the dogs bark and the caravan rolls on. Just learn to roll on. You have more important issues to deal with.

*It is not the critic who counts; not the man who points out how the strong man stumbles, or where the doer of deeds could have done them better. The credit belongs to the man who is actually in the arena, whose face is marred by dust and sweat and blood; who strives valiantly... who at best knows in the end the triumph of high achievement, and who at worst, if he fails, at least fails while daring greatly.*

~Theodore Roosevelt

# The 80/20 Principle

*Waste thrives on complexity—effectiveness
requires simplicity. Whenever something has become complex,
simplify it; if you cannot, eliminate it.*

RICHARD COCH, THE 80/20 PRINCIPLE

IT HAS BEEN SAID THAT THE MASS OF ACTIVITY will always be pointless, poorly conceived, badly directed, wastefully executed, and largely beside the point. Is that discouraging news to you, or is it simply a fact of life?

In 1906, Italian economist Vilfredo Pareto came up with a mathematical formula which explained that 20 percent of the people in his nation owned 80 percent of the land. It wasn't long after he presented this information that people began applying his formula to all areas of life with amazing revelations. His formula was later coined the *80/20 Principle*.

Pareto's 80/20 Principle basically suggests that, for many events, 80 percent of the results come from 20 percent of the causes. Or another way to state it is that *just a few things in life make a big impact, and the rest make little or no difference.*

Listed below are some of the results or impacts that have been suggested:

- 20 percent of inputs account for 80 percent of outputs

- 20 percent of causes produce 80 percent of consequences

- 20 percent of the defects cause 80 percent of the problems in most products

- 20 percent of the work consumes 80 percent of the time and resources

- 20 percent of investors provide 80 percent of the funding
- 20 percent of givers give 80 percent of the money
- 20 percent of criminals commit 80 percent of the crimes
- 20 percent of carpets get 80 percent of the wear
- 20 percent of employees use 80 percent of all sick days
- 20 percent of a blog's posts generate 80 percent of its traffic
- 20 percent of your relationships bring about 80 percent of your joy
- 20 percent of your food choices bring about 80 percent of your health
- 80 percent of a company's revenues are generated by 20 percent of its customers
- 80 percent of complaints come from 20 percent of customers
- 80 percent of happiness is experienced in 20 percent of life

From a practical standpoint, if you worked for ten hours, only two hours of that time would account for the most effective production of your day. The rest of the time would be eaten up by time-wasting activities like paper shuffling (moving one stack to another stack), unnecessary phone calls, reading the paper, extended conversations at the water cooler, surfing the Web for non-business-related information, extended lunch periods and coffee breaks, and pointless meetings that simply waste time and bore people.

So what's the point, you say?

❑ Simplify your objectives, and do the most important 20 percent things you need to do.

❑ When you spot 20-percent-type activity, run to it and immerse yourself in it.

❑ When you get the opportunity, ally yourself with people

who are 20-percent-type thinkers and doers. You need their stimulation and encouragement.

❑ Move 80-percent resources to 20-percent-type activities

❑ Move 20-percent-type individuals away from 80-percent-type activities

❑ Determine to ruthlessly prune your 80-percent activities.

❑ Try to expand your 20-percent activities to 30 percent or 40 percent. What do you think would happen then?

---

*The actions of men are the best interpreters of their thoughts.*

–JOHN LOCKE

# Slippery Slopes

*Whoever fights monsters should see to it that
in the process he doesn't become a monster.*

~Friedrich Nietzsche

IT HAS BEEN SAID THAT IT IS THE FEAR of losing power that corrupts those who wield it—and it is the fear of the scourge of power that corrupts those who are subject to it. William Gaddis said, "Power doesn't corrupt people; people corrupt power."

The abusive behavior and negative influence of those in a position of leadership has been the downfall of nations, organizations, families, and the individual themselves. Corruption begins when those in leadership seek special attention, pursue personal agendas, and attempt to secure favors...all with a strong desire for personal gain. The bottom line of corruption is *selfishness.*

Corruption takes on the form of bribery, nepotism, graft, and a wide range of criminal activity. Corruption deteriorates the trust and confidence of others in everything from world trade, tourism, the achievement of excellence, and the influence of stable and positive role models. Levels of corruption vary according to geographic areas and exist to some degree in all communities worldwide. Corruption has a strong impact on any society. The abuse of entrusted power and authority among leaders is widespread and costly financially and emotionally. The Corruption Perceptions Index is published annually, ranking countries by their perceived level of public sector corruption.

The challenge is to identify and address any level of corruption. The next step is to reduce and eliminate the impact and even the allegations of corruption. The slippery slope of corruption often begins slowly. It starts with neglect to take corrective measures toward what is right and what is wrong. Some leaders believe their wrong actions are not only permissible, but somehow corruption is required for them to succeed. It has been observed that the slippery slope of corrupt leadership can be compared to sheep who "nibble their way lost." Addressing corruption requires the bold, steady step of transparency.

*Corruption is authority, plus monopoly, minus transparency.*

At the top of the list for the causes of corruption are greed and anger. The most prevalent cause, however, is a deficiency in personal character. Any commitment of the leader to address and prevent corruption with integrity and transparency begins with some basic approaches. A leader must have a clearly stated vision. A leader must have a defined set of standards. A leader must seek organizational assessments to identify and correct problem areas. And a leader must accept the responsibility of training for improvement—which includes promoting individual character. It's the leader's responsibility to prepare for challenges, growth, restoration, and a hope for the future.

Why address behavior that leads to corruption? Because doing so reduces conflict, addresses criminal activity, offers an atmosphere of peace and respect, provides greater stability, and earns the trust and confidence of both leaders and followers.

*The corruption of people is to behave in an inhuman way.*

~Alan Bullock

## Accepting the Challenge

Suggested by Marcus Aurelius as imperative for leaders in avoiding corrupt behavior:

*Identifying a conscious and honest purpose for life.* (Character)
*Steady obedience to what is known to be right.* (Integrity)
*An honest estimation of oneself and others.* (Wisdom)
*Frequent self-examination and evaluation.* (Courage)
*Indifference to how others may label you.* (Optimism)

*Corruption is simply crime without conscience.*

~George Marek

# Top 12 Leadership Behaviors—Part I

*Before you are a leader, success is all about growing yourself.*
*When you become a leader, success is all about growing others.*

~JACK WELCH

THE POINTMAN LEADERSHIP INSTITUTE has had the opportunity for 25 years to present leadership seminars in over 70 countries worldwide. They have found a common agreement, regardless of the country, of the top 12 leadership behaviors that followers desire to see in their leaders.

1. **They want leaders to be *decisive*.**
   Making decisions is not always easy, but it's a major responsibility of leaders. Followers don't appreciate wishy-washy, fearful leaders who won't make a decision until they get all the facts. If you wait until you get all the facts, it is no longer a decision...it's a conclusion. Decisions are made without all of the facts. That's why they're called decisions.

   *Nothing is more difficult, and therefore*
   *more precious, than being able to decide.*

   ~NAPOLEON BONAPARTE

2. **They want leaders to be *good listeners*.**
   Followers appreciate leaders who will listen to their opinions, concerns, and even fears. Leaders gain more trust and respect when they are accessible to followers and respect their ideas. Approachability and openness are increased

when the leader walks among the followers while they are
doing their work or if they encourage an open-door policy.

> *Most people do not listen with the intent to understand;*
> *they listen with the intent to reply.*
>
> ~STEPHEN COVEY

### 3. They want leaders to *keep commitments.*

When leaders are dependable, they begin to develop
credibility in the eyes of their followers. The leaders become
believable because they keep their word. Reliability is crucial
for long-term leadership success. Their promises can be
counted on. No one wants to follow someone who does not
tell the truth.

> *If you say something and back it up with your actions, you*
> *will provide the "proof" for people who are listening to*
> *you, and they will much more willingly follow your lead.*
>
> ~JIM ROHN

### 4. They want leaders to be *consistent.*

Consistency in adhering to policies creates a stable working
environment. Leaders who say one thing and behave in a
different manner bring about confusion among followers.
People don't like to work for a leader who is happy one
moment and angry the next. Emotional turmoil destroys
trust and unity.

> *Consistency: It's the jewel worth wearing;*
> *It's the anchor worth weighing;*
> *It's the thread worth weaving;*
> *It's a battle worth winning.*
>
> ~CHARLES SWINDOLL

### 5. They want leaders to display *good judgment.*

No one trusts people who consistently get themselves and
others into trouble. They want to follow a leader who
displays wisdom, insight, and expertise.

*The man who knows right from wrong and has good judgment and common sense is happier than the man who is immensely rich! For such wisdom is far more valuable than precious jewels. Nothing else compares with it. Wisdom gives: a long, good life, riches, honor, pleasure, peace.*

~Proverbs 3:14-17

# Top 12 Leadership Behaviors—Part II

*A leader is one who knows the way, goes the way, and shows the way.*

~JOHN C. MAXWELL

LEADERSHIP BEHAVIORS THAT FOLLOWERS desire to see in their leaders:

6. **They want leaders to be *fair*.**
   The concept of fairness seems to be built into human DNA. Often you hear children and teenagers say, "It isn't fair!" In the workplace, employees are also on the search for fairness in responsibilities, authority, and accountability.

   *Fairness is not an attitude. It's a professional skill*
   *that must be developed and exercised.*

   ~BRIT HUME

7. **They want leaders to *give recognition*.**
   A simple "thank you" is a good place to start. Recognition lets the follower know that they are seen and appreciated. It is important to recognize not only behavior but also the character trait motivating the behavior. Recognition is especially well received when given before a person's peers.

   *I can live for two months on a compliment.*

   ~MARK TWAIN

8. **They want leaders to *remove work barriers*.**
   It is important that leaders eliminate as much paperwork,

red tape, and bureaucracy as possible. Keep the organization, operation, and details simple.

*At least once every five years every form*
*should be put on trial for its life.*

~Peter Drucker

9. **They want leaders to *equip followers*.**
"Carpenters need hammers" and "secretaries need computers" are easy to understand. Every worker needs tools to be the most effective employee possible. Leaders must be alert to the need for equipment, training, and mentoring of all those who follow them.

*A good objective of leadership is to help those*
*who are doing poorly to do well and to help those*
*who are doing well to do even better.*

~Jim Rohn

10. **They want leaders to *emphasize principles and not rules*.**
Rules are necessary to help establish specific boundaries, regulations, guidelines, and procedures. Principles clarify the motivation of why we do what we do.

*Peace of mind comes when your life is in harmony with*
*true principles and values and in no other way.*

~Stephen Covey

11. **They want leaders to be *champions of followers*.**
Followers appreciate it when leaders have their backs and will support them through both the good and bad times. They don't appreciate it when leaders pass the buck, blame the followers for failure, or take credit for any successes.

*Whoever wants to be a leader among you*
*must be your servant* (Matthew 20:26 NLT).

~Jesus of Nazareth

12. **They want leaders to be** *persons of character.*
Your character is what you think about and what you do
when no one is looking.

> *Be more concerned with your character than your reputation,*
> *because your character is what you really are,*
> *while your reputation is merely what others think you are.*
>
> ~JOHN WOODEN

> *And whatever you do in word or deed, do all in the name*
> *of the Lord Jesus, giving thanks to God the Father through Him.*
>
> Colossians 4:17

# Now Hear This!

*Wisdom is the reward you get for a lifetime of
listening when you'd have preferred to talk.*

~Doug Larson

IT HAS BEEN SAID THAT GOD GAVE US TWO EARS and one
mouth so that we would listen more than we speak.

Adler R. Rosenfeld suggests that 70 percent of communication
involves listening, speaking, reading, and writing.

The question is, do we really listen to people when they talk? You see,
it is possible to hear without listening, and you can listen to someone
talk without hearing them. You might hear words spoken but miss the
feelings and heart of the person speaking.

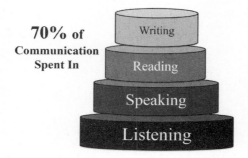

When it comes to listening, we can easily comprehend from 125 to
250 spoken words a minute. We also can think at about 400 to 800
words a minute. This can create a problem if we begin to formulate
responses before the speaker is finished with their thoughts.

*He who answers a matter before he hears*
*it, it is folly and shame to him.*

Proverbs 18:13 NKJV

Barriers to effective listening include a poor environment where there is too much other confusion, distraction, or interruptions. Get to a place where you can communicate without all the interference. You might think of going for a walk or seeking a quiet space. Other barriers could include poor timing and mental, emotional, or physical fatigue with either the speaker or the listener. It's important for the listener not to be preoccupied with the TV, their phone, the computer, personal bias, prejudices, or a negative attitude. The listener must control their urge to talk and remember to be *interested* and not *interesting*. The meeting is not about them.

---

### *Active Listening Involves*

- Facing the speaker, making eye contact, & being alert to body language
- Being interested in them and looking for commonalities
- Let the other person finish speaking before making comments
- Ask questions, nod and make comments, and give feedback
- Listen for content (facts & details), listen for feelings (emotions)
- Acknowledge and validate their feelings as the driving force for concern, conflict, or conduct they are dealing with
- Let go of any agenda you might have and listen for their agenda
- Reflect your reaction, clarify your understanding, summarize what you heard them share and see if they agree with you
- Keep in mind there are always two sides to every issue

**The first one to plead his cause seems right,**
**until his neighbor comes and examines him.**
**Proverbs 18:17**

---

*I only wish I could find an institute that teaches people how to listen.*
*Business people need to listen at least as much as they*
*need to talk. Too many people fail to realize that*
*real communication goes in both directions.*

–LEE IACOCCA

# 26

# Deception

*Sin has many tools, but a lie is the handle which fits them all.*

~OLIVER WENDELL HOLMES

A UNIVERSITY OF MASSACHUSETTS STUDY revealed that 40 percent of those responding lied on resumés. Ninety percent lied on dating profiles, and 54 percent of the time lies could be detected in conversations.

Plato referred to what is known as the "noble lie," which is an untruth spoken to maintain social harmony. Some believe that a lie for the sake of the welfare of others is acceptable.

Why do people lie? Usually, it's because they're feeling guilty about something they did that was not right or good...or something they should have done and did not follow through on. To help cover their "tracks" or the guilt they feel, people will often distract others by making accurate statements with the intent to deceive.

I'm reminded of the story of a lady who made a complaint to police headquarters that a police officer made sexual comments to her. Upon investigation, two policemen were called in to talk about the issue. When the officer in question was asked, "Did you enter the lady's house and make sexual comments to her?" he replied, "I never entered that woman's house."

Then the police officer's partner was asked the same question, "Did your partner enter the woman's house and make sexual comments to her?"

"No sir," was his reply. "He made the sexual comments while standing on her porch." Both officers made accurate statements, but one was deceptive.

Lying can take the form of inflating customer ratings. Remaining silent about poor performance is a form of lying. Denying a program isn't working and allowing it to continue or arranging facts to only point to the best possible view is another form of lying.

Individual lies are then viewed as necessary to avoid embarrassment, unpleasant consequences, and unwanted confrontation. These, of course, are all purely selfish excuses. We pursue lies because we believe it doesn't make us look as guilty. James Garfield reminded us of this when he said, "The truth will set you free, but first it will make you miserable."

Striving for honesty in our day-to-day social actions in both personal and public discourse is essential. Yet, in spite of our best efforts, it can be most challenging. Truthfulness is communicating by life and word that which is genuine and accurate.

How are you doing in the area of truthfulness? When someone calls your office and asks to talk to you, do you tell your secretary or assistant to say, "Tell them I'm not in"? Or, if you have one of the cell phones that tells you who the caller is before answering, it can save you from outright lying. You can pretend that you are not there by not answering the call, and it helps soothe the guilt of your not wanting to talk with that individual. Does this sound familiar?

### Reflections

Is there a truthful way to accomplish what a lie would?
What effect would the lie have on the general rule of telling the truth?
How would an exposed lie look to those closest to you?
How would an exposed lie look to other members of the community?

*I'm not upset you lied to me. I'm upset that*
*from now on I can't believe you.*

-FRIEDRICH NIETZSCHE

# 27

# Keeping Commitments

*Commitment is what transforms a promise into reality.*

~ABRAHAM LINCOLN

**F**AILING TO KEEP COMMITMENTS DISCREDITS and tarnishes our name and leadership. That's a strong statement. What's in a name? Our name is a summary and representation of what we mean to others who are following us. A leader's commitments or lack thereof add personal identity to their names. It's a leader's commitments—especially those that give that sense of total involvement—that motivate and inspire followers.

*There's a difference between interest and commitment. When you're interested in doing something, you do it only when it's convenient. When you're committed to something, you accept no excuses; only results.*

~KENNETH BLANCHARD

One commitment my wife and I made to our family each year was a weeklong family vacation. This was most often at a resort in Northern Minnesota. It involved lakeside cabins, skiing, tubing, fishing, hiking, "bond-fires," and cookouts. This all resulted in a lot of fun and family memories. We always booked the next year's vacation almost immediately after returning home. One particular year presented a last-minute conflict due to a rescheduled criminal trial I was to testify in.

Nonrefundable deposits had been made. Days off from work had been approved. It was not possible to reschedule the reservation for a later time. While it seemed to be a situation where a promise and expectations had to be broken, it was evident that discussion was necessary with attorneys to exhaust all options. Options were shared with the family as a means to keep them informed. Just like planning the vacation and discussing activities is part of building enthusiasm, so is the desire to be careful with our words and commitments by honestly sharing any hurdles and disappointments. Commitments also include doing our part to help realize and overcome obstacles to the best of our ability. The result of my efforts: A pilot was hired to fly me to the trial and back to our vacation. In the end, a plea agreement was reached, and the trial was not necessary.

Think about commitments this way: Commitments are a leader's willingness and promise to give time, energy, and decisions to something they care about and believe in, regardless of the outcome. Highly committed leaders are considered valuable to the vision of the organization and welfare of personnel. Highly committed followers are loyal and often preferred for promotions. Why? Both a leader's and a follower's commitments signify the willing sacrifices that are required in order to turn their words into actions.

I read of a company that, at the end of customer service training for new hires, offered them a $2,000 check to resign and leave. Why? The offer is designed to make sure that those who really are dedicated to staying are actually committed to the promise to represent the values and principles of the organization. How are you doing with your promises and commitments?

### Leadership Tips Learned from Committing to Family Vacations

| | |
|---|---|
| Relationships are grown and stabilized | Conveys value to followers |
| Enhances personal character | Recognizes good work ethic |
| Identifies with trustworthiness | Reduces the need for disputes |
| Helps in becoming a person of your word | Always does more than is expected |

*Commitment is an act, not a word.*

-Jean Paul Sartre

*It was character that got us out of bed, commitment that moved us into action, and discipline that enabled us to follow through.*

~Zig Ziglar

# 28

# Leaders as Coaches

*A lot of people have gone further than they thought*
*they could because someone else thought they could.*

~ZIG ZIGLAR

IN ANCIENT MYTHOLOGY before he left for Troy, Odysseus gave
his son Telemachus into the care of Mentor, whom he entrusted with
looking after Telemachus. Thus, *mentor* became a term associated with
the personal investment of another in order to instruct and encourage.

The idea of mentoring and coaching is simply an interest in another
person's success, well-being, and personal development. Do you possess
such an interest in others? There is a slight difference between coaching
and mentoring. Coaching is task oriented, short term, and performance
driven. Coaching is the ability to empower others to complete duties
and see that their assigned responsibilities are completed.

Mentoring is more relationship oriented, long term, and development
driven. Both are related to the care taken by us as leaders to ensure that
a follower's needs are being served and met. John Whitmore describes
these opportunities for us as "unlocking a person's potential to maximize
their own performance. It is helping them to learn rather than teaching them."

Robert L. Vernon points out that "mentoring involves more than
passing along facts, skills, and techniques. Mentoring transfers values,
principles, ethics, and attitudes. Mentoring is character development."
It takes time and patience for a personal relationship to develop in order
to coach and mentor another person. Can you recall the last time you
served as a coach or mentor?

Coaching and mentoring require good communication. It means
treating others with respect and being aware of our own body language

and tone of voice. Feedback is a significant part of coaching and mentoring. Do not make the feedback personal. Be specific, but do not scold or dictate. Avoid using the "feedback sandwich" of stating an intended negative statement between two positive statements. Address these aspects separately and for the purpose to be served.

As leaders who seek to be coaches and mentors, we have three distinct functions. *Act*—by being advisors and encouragers, while sharing expertise both professionally and personally, without micromanaging. *Guide*—by offering resources, training, and pitching in if and when needed. *Restrain*—by admonishing when needed. Complaints are commonplace, but when complaining words begin to affect behavior, it is always time to step in. As a coach or mentor, consider offering these simple words of affirmation: "I like it." "That's good." "Well done."

*Everybody knows how to utter a complaint,*
*but few can express a graceful compliment.*

~WILLIAM FEATHER

Author Michael Stanier provides suggested questions that can be utilized in developing coaching and mentoring relationships with others. The key is to listen and genuinely acknowledge answers. It's also important to stay informed before committing to a yes or no response.

- "What's on your mind?" A good follow-up question to an answer is "What else?"

- "What challenges are you facing?" A good follow-up question is "What can be done?"

- "What is preventing you from success?" A good follow-up is "What steps are needed?"

- A good feedback question: "What part of our conversation was most beneficial to you?"

*A mentor is someone who sees more talent and ability within*
*you than you see in yourself and helps bring it out of you.*

~ BOB PROCTOR

# 29

# Organizational Assessment

*Progressive improvement beats delayed perfection.*

~Mark Twain

ORWARD-THINKING LEADERS UNDERSTAND there are always ways to improve any organization. They take a figurative step back and evaluate how the organization is operating as a whole. From its current state to its envisioned future, regular organizational assessments impact performance.

Leaders are continually seeking to adapt, influence performance, and survive change. As Peter Drucker has pointed out, "The greatest danger in times of turbulence, is not the turbulence; it is to act with yesterday's logic."

Organizational assessments guide the development of recommendations and action plans to support objectives and enhance overall effectiveness. An organizational assessment is a means—and a tool—that all leaders should utilize in pursuit of continuous improvement for the organization or institution they lead. From nonprofits to Fortune 500 companies, organizational assessments assist in continually striving to determine priorities, make improvements, and allocate resources. Organizational assessments assist leaders and followers alike to perform at maximum effectiveness and highest potential. An organizational assessment needs to be viewed by leaders as a repeatable process to identify needed changes and improved performance levels.

The leader needs to champion the process as relevant, credible, and transparent. Any organizational assessment requires participation at all levels of employment. This helps assure valid information about the conditions of the organization and factors effecting performance.

*Company culture is the product of a company's*
*values, expectations, and environment.*

~COURTNEY CHAPMAN

Independent analysis sources utilize: 1) site visits, 2) policy review, 3) interviews, and 4) surveys aimed at anonymity of communication and accountability of the needs and training of all followers. While some question the validity of self-assessments, they go a long way toward encouraging ownership, fostering honest feedback and personal commitment, and serving internally to develop leaders at all levels.

Organizational assessments simply seek information in order to learn what impacts and improves the organization overall. There are a number of models to choose from. The pattern and purpose are generally consistent...each with specific dimensions to help improve any organization. When was the last time you did an organizational assessment of your business?

*An organization's ability to learn, and transform that learning*
*into action rapidly, is the ultimate competitive advantage.*

~JACK WELCH

# Organizational Assessment Tool

*Organizational assessment is a framework for improving performance.*

~INTERNATIONAL DEVELOPMENT RESEARCH CENTER

ORGANIZATIONAL CONSULTANT GARRY BROWN suggests strategic leadership helps the organization stay on course with its mission. Here are six specific dimensions that can help improve the organization. Be as objective as you can in answering each dimension question using this five-point scale:

**1.** Needs major improvement  **2.** Some improvement needed
**3.** Adequate  **4.** Above average  **5.** Superior

### Direction:

\_\_\_\_ Does the organization have a clear vision, mission, and purpose?

\_\_\_\_ Does staff know, understand, and live the mission?

\_\_\_\_ Is the vision idealistic, challenging, and inspiring?

\_\_\_\_ Do the mission and purpose statements answer why the organization exists?

\_\_\_\_ Are there identified, specific goals and objectives to accomplish over the next year?

### Teamwork:

\_\_\_\_ Does staff work together in a complementary and supportive way?

\_\_\_\_ Is there competition, bickering, and "buck passing"?

\_\_\_\_ Are personal interests sacrificed for the welfare of individual teams?

_____ Do decisions made consider the impact on other entities in the organization?

_____ Is there fragmentation and compartmentalized thinking?

## Staff Development:

_____ Does all staff have the opportunity to reach their potential?

_____ Are staff given sufficient training to ensure completed work assignments?

_____ Does staff have the opportunity to learn from senior members?

_____ Does staff have the opportunity for career development or differing responsibilities?

_____ Is timely, objective information provided to staff regarding personal achievements?

## Principles, Values, and Policies:

_____ Are they known, discussed, enforced, and part of the organizational culture?

_____ Are the principles foundational, basic, unchangeable truths?

_____ Are the principles valued enough to be reinforced though rewards and sanctions?

_____ Do the operational policies provide a definite course or method of action?

_____ Do the policies provide guidance in accordance with the values and principles?

## Communication:

_____ Is there a free flow of thoughts and ideas among leaders and followers?

_____ Are goals, priorities, and opinions freely shared?

_____ Do other departments have an exchange and flow of concerns and problems?

_____ Do meetings have an advanced agenda, and are they generally viewed as productive?

_____ Are decisions made and responsibilities assigned with due dates?

## Controls:

\_\_\_\_\_ Are policies published, discussed, and understood?
\_\_\_\_\_ Are there procedures to ensure execution of work done?
\_\_\_\_\_ Is staff accountable, rewarded, and sanctioned fairly?
\_\_\_\_\_ Is the vision pursued and the mission being accomplished?
\_\_\_\_\_ Are organizational values esteemed and lived out?

In addition to self-assessment, leaders may find it useful to pass out this assessment to their followers. If not satisfied with the results, seek assistance in achieving measurable results.

*To win in the market, you must first win in the work place.*

–Douglas Grant

*Don't lower your expectations to meet your performance.*
*Raise your level of performance to meet your expectations.*

–Ralph Marston

# 31

# Victims and Victors

*Let us resolve to be masters, not the victims, of our history,
controlling our own destiny without giving way to
blind suspicions and emotions.*

~JOHN F. KENNEDY

IN THE 1950s, JULIAN B. ROTTER SUGGESTED a concept called *locus of control*. The word *locus* refers to a location or site, which becomes the center or starting point of action. At the locus or starting point, an individual could choose two courses of thought. They could choose to believe that *external* events, circumstances, or people in our lives determine or control outcomes. Or they could choose to believe the outcomes in our lives are determined or brought about by our *internal* thoughts, decisions, and actions.

At one extreme is the belief our lives are controlled by fate, the stars, or good and bad luck. At the other extreme, our lives are determined by our choices and hard work. We can each say, "I am the captain of my soul."

| External Control | Internal Control |
| --- | --- |
| Blame others for actions | Take responsibility for actions |
| More influenced by others' opinions | Less influenced by others' opinions |
| Tasks completed under direction | Task oriented at their own pace |
| Lower self-image | Stronger self-image |
| Less goal oriented | More goal oriented |
| Overwhelmed with challenges | Confident with challenges |
| Tend toward health issues | Often physically healthier |
| Lean toward sadness | Lean toward happiness |
| Display dependence on others | Display independence from others |
| More pessimistic | More optimistic |

Somewhere between no control and absolute control we live our lives. Those who have absolute control can become tyrants. If we give up all control, we lean toward anarchy. External circumstances can provide opportunities for us by being in the right place at the right time. Opportunity often knocks dressed in work clothes. However, we may not be aware of the knocking because we're in the backyard looking for four-leaf clovers to bring us luck...or at least filling out the Publisher's Clearing House Sweepstakes envelope.

The term *locus of control* is not used as often as it used to be. The term *external control* has now been replaced with "*You're a victim*" of people and circumstances. And the term *internal control* is now expressed as "*You're a victor*" by making your own decisions and creating circumstances for success.

Where do you see yourself today? Are you alert to the attitudes and beliefs of those who work under you? Do you need to make some movement on the scale? Do those under you need some help and encouragement? You are not only responsible for your decisions and actions...your followers are looking to you to set an example.

> *We who lived in concentration camps can remember the men who walked through the huts comforting others, giving away their last piece of bread. They may have been few in number, but they offer sufficient proof that everything can be taken away from a man but one thing: the last of the human freedoms—to choose one's attitude in any given set of circumstances, to choose one's own way.*
>
> ~Viktor E. Frankl

# 32

# Regrets

*Of all sad words of tongue or pen, the saddest are these,*
*"It might have been."*

~John Greenleaf Whittier

HAVE YOU EVER FELT SHAME FOR SOMETHING you said or did? The shame we feel for any wrong is painful (that's on the negative side). On the positive side, if shame hurts enough, it will keep us from repeating the same thing a second time. It's like when we get an expensive ticket for speeding. It's painful, and it doesn't feel good. However, the financial pain is a reminder that we don't want to go through that experience another time.

Shame also has another negative side effect. It often drives us toward an emotion called regret. We all have regrets in life; however, regret has never paid any debt. Regret does not have the power to change anything. It's just a weight that hangs about our neck. It hinders us from changing and moving forward. It keeps us in a sad mood all the time.

Regret has a tendency to create worry, anxiety, depression, and anger. Anxiety is basically fear about future events—what's going to happen in the days ahead? Depression involves hurt and anger over past events involving people and situations. We can also be angry with ourselves.

There's a thread that runs through anxiety and depression. The thread is called *control*. We wish we could control our future. We also wish we had control over our past. Guess what? We have no control over the future or the past. We have to let go of the control and give it to God.

Regret is similar to ripping scabs off a wound that's trying to heal. Scab ripping occurs when we keep revisiting the entire situation over and over again, thereby ripping open the emotional wound. It's very difficult for a wound to heal when I keep ripping the scab off—sometimes as a punishment to myself. Is scab ripping working for you?

We don't have control of other people ripping our scabs off and exposing the wound. We just have to endure and continue on. We do have control of our own personal habit of opening up the wound—thinking that beating ourselves up will somehow help erase what we said or did.

There is a difference between problems and facts of life. A problem is something you can work on and change. A fact of life is something you can't change. You just simply have to accept the fact and make the best of an unpleasant situation.

*Make it a rule of life never to regret and never to look back.*
*Regret is an appalling waste of energy; you can't build on it;*
*it's only good for wallowing in.*

~Katherine Mansfield

So, where do you think you should spend your time—regretting the past, or making course corrections so you will not keep on saying or doing things you will regret? Your past is only a memory, and you cannot change it. You only have today to make changes. Stop the wallowing. Admit and own your wrongs. Make a commitment to change. Attempt to reconcile or make restitution if possible. Begin a new future. Today is the beginning of the rest of your life.

*Regret for time wasted can become a power for good in the time that*
*remains, if we will only stop the waste and the idle, useless regretting.*

~Arthur Brisbane

# Right Words

*The right word spoken is a precious rarity.*

~JOHN O'REILLY

WHAT IS THE IMPACT OF OUR WORDS upon those we have influence over? Leaders tend to be known by what they say and the particular words they choose to say. The words selected can be received as either positive or negative. Words have energy and power, with the ability to help and heal, as well as to harm or humiliate. They can be piercing words, self-serving words, and words that are false. It has been said that sharp words make more wounds than surgeons can heal.

Or we can choose encouraging words, comforting words, and words that are true. While right words can show conviction, other words carelessly stated can cause fear. Words matter. Words are not neutral. Humans are built for words. We have a need for words. Words are receiver oriented. Whether spoken or written, a leader's words have a significant impact to create lasting memories on those they lead.

Unfortunately, leaders of many cultures tend to have a growing loss of restraint in what they say. If you're in leadership, good communication is a must. It has been said that 85 percent of a leader's success is based on their ability to communicate. The words we elect to use are giving our followers a reason to listen, a reason to trust, and a reason to experience a more positive outlook for the future. However, this is true of not just leaders. Everyone needs to monitor what they say and how they say it. A good example would be instead of calling someone "stupid," it might be better to say that they are "reckless" in their actions. Negative comments can be made worse by adding profanity with them.

John Piper concluded that these "throw-in words" to try and help make a point are a reflection of a sinful nature, always working to diminish other people's character and our own.

*The words of his mouth were smoother than*
*butter, but war was in his heart; his words were*
*softer than oil, yet they were drawn swords.*

~Psalm 55:21 NKJV

A 2006 Northern Illinois study revealed that swearing is a way of attempting to get attention and communicate "you are the most important person in the room." Words are most definitely a direct reflection of our personal character.

None of us are as word perfect as we would like to be. A leader should desire to use words that are practical, specific, and positive in order to express to another person the underlying need they have for being valued. Our words actually stimulate the minds of others and connect us to them. Mark Twain said it quite well: "The difference between the right word and the almost right word is really a large matter. It is the difference between the lightning bug and the lightning."

A couple good questions to ask ourselves are these: "Does what I am about to say have—or will it add—value?" "Can I get my message across without embellishing the 'sensory words' that sidetrack or destroy the leadership I'm attempting to establish?"

### Words That Are Practical, Specific, and Positive...

Are aimed at being curious instead of frustrated.

Are aimed at helping connect well before reacting.

Are aimed at developing respect, self-control, and patience.

Are aimed at an underlying need of expressing longing value.

Are aimed at what to refrain from, more than what to express.

Are aimed at a purposeful connection of equal speaking and listening.

Are aimed at communicating with not only the mind, but the heart also.

Are aimed at the desire to understand and share in the feelings of another.

*The words of the reckless pierce like swords,*
*but the tongue of the wise brings healing.*

~Proverbs 12:18 NIV

# In Authority, Under Authority

*When leaders lead right, followers follow well.*

A UTHORITY IS IMPORTANT TO THE SUCCESS of any social or religious organization. Some system of authority is required for all communal living. Authority is most often recognized in the branches of the military and policing professions. Authority is also seen in homes with parents, in schools with teachers, and in work with employers. It's common to look at outward signs of authority like education, title, and position. It's equally important to look at the inward signs of authority that validate a leader having authority over others. For instance, compare Adolf Hitler to Mother Teresa. I know— a 180-degree difference. Here's the point: Both had instruction, experience, and opportunity. The difference is found in their actions, based on their motives, through the authority they recognized over them, in order to demonstrate their own influence.

In his book *Animal Farm*, George Orwell relates a story of authority through an allegorical tale of farm animals. The animals take on the traits of human beings in ruling over the farm. Orwell addresses the effects of power and corruption that follow the abuse of legitimate authority. The story reveals that authority without character leads to power without respect. Claiming to have the right to authority, but showing a significant lack of what is morally permissible and right, is an obvious abuse of that authority. The result...a rebellious attitude in others. Legitimate authority should seek a strong followership as an outcome of sound ethical principles and excellence of character in the leader. Orwell's story is also said to support Lord Acton's statement: "Power tends to corrupt. Absolute power corrupts absolutely." Take time to read this story. Which character do you find yourself relating to?

With all authority comes the right to make decisions, give direction, and require obedience. Any abuse of authority can lead to injustice, oppression, and violence. Leaders can use power to restrain destructive impulses or to lie, control, and harm others. It's common for leaders who abuse power to be the most rigorous asserters of it. Do you take a certain pride and pleasure in anything that exercises control over others? As ethical leaders, we must be prepared to serve in ways that reject this concept.

While respecting positions of authority, we should never blindly accept authority by turning a blind eye to dishonest or fraudulent conduct. Have you experienced this? We all have the right to question, "Under whose authority?" when we think the power exercised is unfounded or unjust. I believe any question of the validity of any given authority must answer this question. Does abiding by my immediate authority violate a higher authority, my conscience, or absolute moral law? It also requires a self-check of our motives. Our human tendency is to rebel against any authority, ranging from parents, to coaches, to presidents. In doing so, are we seeking what is good, right, and safe? Or is it an attempt to bring a leader into disrepute with others? It does happen. Deserved respect is replaced with a prideful attitude of "You can't tell me what to do!" Are you prepared to respond based on an identified guiding principle, or do you simply want to argue your preference? If we question authority, we must be prepared to provide a reason for it, an answer to it, or a solution for it.

Those in *legitimate authority* will not ask followers to do anything illegal, immoral, or unethical, or unnecessarily and recklessly choose to violate the health and safety of others. A leader in authority is a leader under authority. It's putting others before yourself with the ability to recognize a higher authority than yourself and submitting to it.

## Key Concepts

Authority exercised justly leads to loyal followers.

# Leadership Know-How

*Consider the questions below in relation to your leadership needs and responsibilities. Place a check in the box if it applies to you or is an area you need to work on.*

❑ **Are you willing to give up your private time for others?**

- ○ *Meetings are highly overrated as a way to build commitment; it is in individual conversations that you earn the right to lead others.*

- ○ *We all find time to do what we really want to do.*—William Feather

❑ **Are you willing to learn how to become a better leader?**

- ○ *Management is doing things right; leadership is doing the right things.*—Peter Drucker

- ○ *The ultimate responsibility of a leader is to facilitate other people's development as well as his own.*—Fred Pryor

❑ **Will you take time to give praise and say thank-you?**

- ○ *You must not pay a person a compliment, and then straightway follow it with a criticism.*—Mark Twain

❑ **Do you have the ability to deal with conflict?**

- ○ *When we apply the hot water of life, we'll see what's in your tea bag.*

- ○ *If death and taxes are the first two certainties of life, conflict is the third.*

- ○ *A leader who will not confront is not a leader.*

- ○ *In conflict, never confront power with power. Always confront power with truth.*

❑ **Are you willing to face the loneliness of the position?**

 ○ *The whole conviction of my life now rests upon the belief that loneliness, far from being a rare and curious phenomenon, peculiar to myself and a few other solitary men, is the central and inevitable fact of human existence.*—Thomas Wolfe

❑ **Can you handle the stress of decision-making?**

 ○ *What separates slow, unproductive leaders from rapid, highly productive leaders? It is the ability to process information and make decisions.*

 ○ *Be willing to make decisions. That's the most important quality in a good leader. Don't fall victim to what I call the Ready-Aim-Aim-Aim Syndrome. You must be willing to fire.*—T. Boone Pickens

❑ **Are you willing to lead in uncharted territory?**

 ○ *Many live in dread of what is coming. Why should we? The unknown puts adventure into life... The unexpected around the corner gives a sense of anticipation and surprise. Thank God for the unknown future.*—E. Stanley Jones

❑ **Do you have a genuine appreciation for others?**

 ○ *The deepest principle in human nature is the craving to be appreciated.*—William James

 ○ *I have yet to find a man, whatever his situation in life, who did not do better work and put forth greater effort under a spirit of approval than he ever would do under a spirit of criticism.*—Charles M. Schwab

❑ **Are you able to recognize initiative and acknowledge credit to others?**

 ○ *Initiative consists of doing the right thing without being told.*—Irving Mack

 ○ *He who seizes the right moment, is the right man.*—Johann Goethe

# Parkinson's Law

*The man who is denied the opportunity of taking decisions of importance begins to regard as important the decisions he is allowed to take. He becomes fussy about filing, keen on seeing that pencils are sharpened, eager to ensure that the windows are open (or shut) and apt to use two or three different-colored inks.*

~C. Northcote Parkinson

I'M SURE YOU HAVE BEEN EXPOSED TO PARKINSON'S LAW, which states: "Work expands so as to fill the time available for its completion."

A number of years ago I came into the office and gathered the various secretaries together for a short meeting. I asked them how heavy their workload was for that particular day. They all groaned a little and proceeded to inform me that it was quite large, and they didn't know if they could complete it all.

I apologized and said, "I'm so sorry. I didn't know your workload was so big. I had planned to tell you that you could all go home early at 2:00 p.m. if you could get it completed."

A startling thing happened. The groaning all stopped. They all looked at each other and said, "We think we can get it done by 2:00 p.m." It was amazing—they got the work done.

Parkinson's Law has spawned a number of corollaries:

- Work complicates to fill the available time.

- If you wait until the last minute, it only takes a minute to do.

- Work contracts to fit in the time we give it.

- In ten hours a day, you have time to fall twice as far behind your commitments as in five hours a day.

- Data expands to fill the space available for storage.

- The amount of time that someone has to perform a task is the amount of time it will take to complete the task.

- Parkinson's Fourth Law: The number of people in any working group tends to increase regardless of the amount of work to be done.

To fight against the effects of Parkinson's Law, you have to first acknowledge that it's affecting you. Next, it would be good to ask, "*Why* is it present in my life? Am I bored? Do I not want to do a particular task, and I'm just putting it off? Is it because I don't want to talk with a certain person?"

In practical terms, it might be good to set realistic limits on the time it takes for the completion of certain tasks. It might be good to even cut that time back somewhat to help put a little pressure on yourself. You could also:

- Set limits on the amount of money you are going to spend.

- Limit the size of your food servings and use smaller plates.

- Set deadlines for writing. I've been asked, "How do you deal with writer's block when ideas don't come?" My response is simple: "I don't have writer's block because I've got deadlines. It's got to come whether I like it or not."

- Get organized and get rid of all the clutter. This is not a one-time task. It's a continual process of throwing away things you'll never use. They're just in the way.

- Set timers for reminders, prioritize various tasks to be completed, divide large tasks into smaller tasks, and reward yourself for beating your deadlines.

If you knew that you were going to die, would it help you to focus on how you spent your time? Would it help you to focus on what is truly important in a given day? Guess what? You are going to die. That thought will help you to use time wisely.

# Truthfulness

*Truthfulness is the main element of character.*
*Truthfulness is the real mark of integrity.*

~Brian Tracy

"THE STATE CALLS OFFICER WALINGA TO THE STAND." Words I had heard before from the prosecuting attorney. I made my way from the spectator seating to stand before the judge's bench. "Raise your right hand," said the judge. I did. He continued, "Do you swear to tell the truth, the whole truth, and nothing but the truth?" he asked, pausing, awaiting my response. "I do, so help me, God," I answered. "Take a seat," he said, as he motioned for me to take my place in the witness box.

Following my testimony and cross-examination by the defense attorney, the judge called for a short recess. He also requested that I meet with him in the judge's chambers. Once in his chambers, the judge began.

"Officer Walinga, you simply need to respond with 'I do' to taking an oath in my courtroom."

"Yes, sir, I was just surprised when you didn't finish with 'so help you, God,'" I replied.

"What do you mean?" he asked.

"Well, sir, I have never experienced an incomplete oath before," I said.

"What do you mean 'incomplete'?" he asked.

"Well, sir, in all my years as an officer, God's name has always been used as the highest authority recognized in any commitment to testify truthfully in a court of law," I replied.

The response came quickly. "That may be, Officer Walinga, but in my courtroom I am the highest authority." So much for challenging a judge.

In the history of court oaths, attaching God's name to lies, half-truths, or ill-conceived purposes is perjury. Invoking the name of God as a divine witness regarding our truthful words, actions, and behaviors is an ultimate promise and act of accountability. Telling the truth represents a desire to maintain order, promote authenticity, and identify with the legitimacy of authority.

With words or on paper, our actions represent promises to certain terms, conditions, and expectations. Far too often, when the terms or conditions are no longer convenient, leaders renege on those commitments. And tragically, trust is broken all too often with seeming abandon.

It's easy to express sentiments of truth like loyalty, respect, and love. But what happens when truthfulness costs you something like your time, money, or reputation? How about when you face difficulty or failure? Is truth still a priority for you? Is truth still the mark of an honorable person and leader? Does truth still matter? Is it true that you grow and mature from mistakes? Do you admit when you are wrong? Is it true that relationships are established and grow on honesty? Are you honest in your relationships? Is it true that lying and hypocrisy break down institutions and organizations? Is there any dishonesty in your organization?

The truth is, people are more likely to follow a leader whose actions match their stated beliefs. Truthful leaders seek to avoid divided loyalties by saying different things to different people about the same situation.

Truthful leaders allow followers to know them as consistent and predictable. Truthful leaders reflect the character of speech that gives the listeners free choice to decide. Truthful leaders do not allow a secret indulgence to undermine their organizational witness. In short, you cannot turn truth on and off like a lightbulb. Is your switch on or off?

# Are Leaders Born or Made?

*Give me anyone but a schizophrenic and I'll turn him into a leader.*

~GENERAL DAVE PALMER

THE ABOVE HEADING IS THE MOST BASIC and often-asked question about leadership from around the world. The short answer is...yes. However, some researchers will even go farther, offering an estimation to answer this question by stating that leadership is about one-third born and two-thirds made. I believe it is fair to say that the majority of leadership is developed in each individual.

If you visit any school playground in any country, you will soon notice which of the young boys and girls are demonstrating leadership qualities. Who is the person organizing the recess activity? Who is the person willing to be the team captain? Who is the person clarifying the rules and settling a dispute over who is "safe" and who is "out"? (Not always to everyone's liking.) What leadership classes did they attend as a grade school youngster?

There is no doubt that, at any age, the quality trait of being assertive is advantageous to leadership. But as growth and maturity take place, those desiring to be leaders also need to understand the processes and concepts of leadership. They need to balance leadership with character traits and the ability to control their behavior. This combination is referred to as social intelligence. Not in the sense of a person's individual IQ, but in the sense of a greater understanding for the role of oneself and of others in the sphere of our influence as a leader.

Whether viewed as more of a natural leader or a learned leader, there is a good chance that leadership has also been modeled in the life of that person. Someone who they would like to emulate has impacted them—maybe a father, an uncle, or a coach. Yet, even a person with limited exposure to leadership or overexposure to poor leadership—but having a desire to be a good leader—can still succeed. How? It takes self-discipline through learning, training, and experience to become a leader with the ability to succeed in influencing others.

*That some have succeeded is proof that others can as well.*

~ABRAHAM LINCOLN

King David is a biblical example of a developing leader. David was not satisfied with obtaining a level of competence and then choosing to stop trying to improve. David was human and erred, but he was willing to keep learning. He served 40 years as king. Examine the partial list of examples below of both personal development and skill development competencies in order to continue achieving your goals as a leader.

| Personal Development | Skill Development |
|---|---|
| ❑ Character | ❑ Accountability |
| ❑ Values | ❑ Short-range planning |
| ❑ Purpose | ❑ Human resources |
| ❑ Resilience | ❑ Team building |
| ❑ Passion | ❑ Decision-making |
| ❑ Vision | ❑ Communication |
| ❑ Wisdom | ❑ Stewardship |
| ❑ Priorities | ❑ Time management |
| ❑ Risk taking | ❑ Organization |
| ❑ Commitments | ❑ Research |
| ❑ Confidence | ❑ Scheduling |
| ❑ Dedication | ❑ Goal setting |

## *Leadership Thought*

There is a need for good leadership in society, in homes, in businesses, in churches, in organizations, and in government.

If the desire and ability to lead is evident, both personal development and skill development are needed. And both are a lifelong process. Are you ready to put forth the effort to become an effective leader?

# 39

# Stealing Property

*Among the natural rights of the Colonists are these;*
*First a right to life, second to liberty; and third to property.*
*Together, with the right to defend them in the best manner they can.*

~SAMUEL ADAMS

I N LATTER DRAFTS OF THE DECLARATION OF INDEPEN-
DENCE, the phrase "pursuit of happiness" was used in place of "property" for the three inalienable rights. This was mainly done because it
removed the inference of a person as slave property. And secondly, it promoted education and the advancing of oneself through learning. "Pursuit of happiness" represented a life that was able to fulfill the needs of
personal knowledge as well a material property—as long as it did not
violate the rights of others. A political system that exploits others, such
as communism and socialism, discredits this important concept. Criss
Jami reminds us that "Man is not by nature deserving of all that he wants.
When we think we are automatically entitled to something, that is when
we start walking all over others to get it." This is a slippery slope.

The regard for property did not just refer to owning land. It included
personal goods or items. The expected right was for all persons to be
secure with their property and to be granted privacy. This right goes
beyond outright stealing or vandalism. Whether intellectual or physical,
inherited or through hard work, everyone can agree that the regard for
property is essential for any society.

Consider the following examples of violating ownership and the use
of deceptive forms of stealing:

| | | |
|---|---|---|
| Copyright violations | Faulty weights | Not returning items |
| Deceiving stockholders | Frivolous lawsuits | Piracy of software |
| Defaulting on a loan | Inflated appraisals | Selling defective goods |
| Extended coffee breaks | Inflated prices | Taking small items |
| Excessive interest | Insurance fraud | Untrue time sheets |
| False expense reports | Low employee wages | Wasting time at work |

Plato cautions us: "He who steals a little, steals with the same wish as he who steals a lot, but with less power." Carmen Ortiz noted quite accurately, "Stealing is stealing whether you use a computer command or a crowbar, and whether you take documents, data, or dollars."

You may have heard the story of the farmer who finds a young boy sitting under an apple tree in his orchard. "Young man, are you trying to steal some of my apples?" asked the farmer. "No, sir," replied the young boy, "I'm trying not to." How about the story of the man who found a large bank deposit of cash on the sidewalk and turned it over to a bank teller? When asked why he did not keep it, the man responded "My conscience would be troubled, and I decided I just couldn't live with a thief."

Keep in mind, jealousy and envy are root causes of violations of property rights. Envy is the desire for someone else's possessions. Jealousy is the insecurity of not having enough possessions. An example of envy is when someone watches another person succeed and feels resentment about their success. They may also feel jealous because they too wanted or desired the same type of success. Jealousy and envy are next-door neighbors to stealing and lying. How are you doing in respecting the property of others? Does your conscience bring anything to mind that you need to deal with?

I'm reminded of the story of the man who left work with a wheelbarrow full of sand for 30 days in a row. The security guards sifted through the sand to see if he was stealing something. They found nothing. At the end of the month, one of the man's friends asked him if he was stealing sand from his company. He said, "Of course not. I'm taking wheelbarrows."

# 40

# Faults, Flaws, and Failings

*It is very easy to forgive others their mistakes. It takes more grit
and gumption to forgive them for having witnessed your own.*

~JESSAMYN WEST

EARTHQUAKES ARE COMMON IN MANY PARTS of the
world. They produce rumblings and loud noise and a dangerous
shaking of foundations. Sometimes they create faults or cracks in the
ground, which can be dangerous. Earthquakes can range from mild to
quite severe.

In a similar way, faults in leadership can range from mild to quite
severe. They can produce rumblings of discontent, a dangerous shaking of relationships, and cracks in the foundation of a healthy business.
Listed below are some dangerous leadership earthquakes.

Turn on your leadership seismograph and become alert to dangerous
vibrations and possible faults that could occur in your leadership. Stop
them before they start.

- ❑ **Blowing up**—Some leaders are a walking time bomb. They
  have frustrations, impatience, and anger that they love to
  share. They're usually equal opportunity providers. They
  love to share their negative spirit not only with employees,
  but also with family, friends, and sometimes customers.
  They have a secret trip wire that causes them to explode at
  the most inappropriate times; however, no one knows what
  actually sets them off.

- ❑ **Changing targets**—Have you ever licked your finger
  and then held it up to see which way the wind was blowing? Some leaders have constantly wet fingers because the

wind is always changing direction. A double-minded leader makes it difficult to stay on course. Is your finger wet or dry?

❑ **Failure to break down silos**—Silos refer to tall, round structures built to store and protect foods like grain and corn. Silos in a company refer to organizational and departmental structures created not to protect grain but to safeguard ideas, methods, and territorial space. Their creation occurs when one department is unwilling to communicate or work with another department. Unity and teamwork are just concepts, not reality. It's time to get out your sledgehammer and go to work.

❑ **The 30,000-Foot Syndrome**—This is a common disease affecting too many leaders. This infection starts when leaders begin to believe their role is to remain in the high clouds of vision and the big picture. It is beneath them to descend out of the loftiness of being on top of the pyramid of work and become involved in mundane details and everyday tasks. They might become infected with a germ of reality, which infects lowly workers. Where's the hypodermic needle of common sense?

❑ **Not walking the talk**—This is another common disease infecting many in leadership. It springs forth out of the "Do-as-I-say-and-not-as-I-do Syndrome." It often hampers the leader from executing strategic plans, seeking advice or counsel, which everyone should do but them, and working a full eight-hour day like everyone in the company was hired to do. God forbid they should become an example for everyone to follow.

❑ **Monkey business**—This is the serious business of listening to everyone's problems and difficulties and being the all-wise counselor. They must seek to become the only one who can solve all the issues. This leader must be able to take the "monkey problems" off of everyone else's backs and carry them for those who cannot and will not solve their own issues. It's important that they become famous for their strong gift of caring. Feel free to bring them any issue so they can take on the responsibility and relieve you of any accountability.

# 41

# It's Up Time, America!

*The greatest discovery of any generation is that a human being can alter his life by altering his attitude.*

~William James

THE FOLLOWING PRESENTATION was given by Kimberly Alyn, a friend and coauthor of *How to Deal with Annoying People*:

- It's time for this country to experience a little up time...so, LISTEN UP, AMERICA.
- If you see injustice, STAND UP.
- If something needs to be said, SPEAK UP.
- If you make an appointment, SHOW UP.
- If you're blind to your faults, WAKE UP.
- If you make a mistake, FESS UP.
- If you're overstepping, BACK UP.
- If you get behind, CATCH UP.
- If they knock you down, GET UP.
- If you're out of line, STRAIGHTEN UP.
- When your boss instructs, KEEP UP.
- When your elders speak, LISTEN UP.
- When your teachers teach, SIT UP.
- When your preachers preach, OWN UP.
- When your country calls, MAN UP.
- Ladies too...WOMAN UP.
- When the fight is over, MAKE UP.
- If you're being hard, EASE UP.
- If your heart is closed, OPEN UP.

- If you want to buy something, SAVE UP.
- It's not an entitlement, so SHUT UP.
- If you make a mess, CLEAN IT UP.
- If you drop trash, PICK IT UP.
- If a car is waiting for you to walk across the street, SPEED IT UP.
- If you're cold busted, GIVE IT UP.
- If people fall down, HELP THEM UP.
- Not the government, YOU STEP UP.
- No bailouts, so PONY UP.
- It's the American way, so CLEAN IT UP.
- If idiots start fighting, BREAK IT UP.
- If the music is wholesome, TURN IT UP.
- If the message is poisonous, THROW IT UP.
- If your words are vulgar, CLAM IT UP.
- If your words encourage, KEEP IT UP.
- If your pants are baggy, PULL THEM UP.
- If your belt's too loose, CINCH IT UP.
- If your fly is down, ZIP IT UP.
- If you're dressed half naked, COVER IT UP.
- If you can't afford stuff, PASS IT UP.
- And you can take your whining and PACK IT UP.
- It's called personal responsibility, SO TAKE IT UP.
- If you make a promise, BACK IT UP.
- This country was founded on it, so you can LOOK IT UP.
- It's the American way, people, so TURN IT UP.
- If life gets boring, you can SHAKE IT UP.
- If life is good, you SOAK IT UP.
- If life is unfair, you SUCK IT UP.
- If life is funny, you can YUCK IT UP.
- If life is sad, just look STRAIGHT UP.
- And life is too short, so people, LIVE IT UP.

# 42

# Attitude

*Keep your thoughts positive because your thoughts become your words.*
*Keep your words positive because your words become your behavior.*
*Keep your behavior positive because your behavior becomes your habits.*
*Keep your habits positive because your habits become your values.*
*Keep your values positive because your values become your destiny.*

~MAHATMA GANDHI

WHEN EVERYTHING IS GOING RIGHT, it's easy to have a positive mental attitude. When things go wrong, we can experience a multitude of negative thoughts. Our emotions can range from anger at one end to fear at the other end. This is basically the fight (anger) or flight (fear) syndrome.

Let's break the attitude process down a little. What makes up or determines our attitude? It's a mix of a number of things. Our attitude is made up of our beliefs, values, observations, opinions, and emotions. Those five factors are then mixed together with facts, events, experiences, relationships, and circumstances. Those ten items are the building blocks for either a positive or a negative attitude.

There's a story of two workers who were asked what they were doing. The first responded, "I'm down in a trench laying blocks for the foundation of this building." The second man in the trench replied, "I'm building a church." Both were in the trench. Both were working. Both were experiencing the same thing. Both had a different perspective after evaluation of the same facts. Both had a choice to respond to the same thing they were doing. What made the difference? Attitude and outlook.

There was a man named Paul who experienced many difficulties. They were harsh and very unpleasant. In fact, they were very painful physically and emotionally.

- He was put in jail on a number of occasi[ons]
- He was beaten five times with thirty-nine [...] whip.
- He was beaten three times with wooden rod[s]
- He spent a day and night swimming in the oc[ean]
- He experienced floods, robbers, and angry mo[bs]
- He was weary from travel and sleepless nights.
- He was often hungry and thirsty, and shivered with cold without warm clothing.
- He experienced constant worry and sadness in relationships.

If anyone had a right to a negative attitude, it would certainly have been Paul. He didn't have a life of ease. With all of these facts, events, and circumstances going on in his life, how did he respond? What was his attitude?

*Always be full of joy in the Lord...Don't worry about anything...pray about everything...Fix your thoughts on what is true and good and right. Think about things that are pure and lovely, and dwell on the fine, good things in others. Think about all you can praise God for and be glad about. Keep putting to practice all you learned from me and saw me doing, and the God of peace will be with you.*

~Philippians 4:4-9

*How's your attitude today? What are you focusing on?*

# Planning for Life

*Most people don't plan to fail; they fail to plan.*

~John L. Beckley

IT HAS BEEN SAID THAT PLANNING FOR LIFE is like navigation. It really isn't so hard if you know where you are and where you want to go. Planning for life simply takes thought and time.

Some of the earliest history of cultures has revealed documentation supporting the need to plan for life. In 1000 BC, expenses connected with death were provided through advance collections. In AD 1600, England formed "Lloyds of London Coffee House" to insure mariners. Benjamin Franklin was instrumental in 1759 in establishing the first life insurance company as a benefit for pastors. The New York Stock Exchange was established in 1792 to initially trade government securities. Then in 1905, U.S. president Teddy Roosevelt investigated corruption and the need for reform and regulations. We can be thankful for the legislation, principles, and safeguards that continue today.

Interestingly, a majority of alleged fraud cases reported and investigated are from uninformed clients. It's not wise to put your money into a product you do not understand. It's far better for you to make a timely, informed decision than a quick, symbolic commitment based on someone else deciding what is best for you.

Whether you have been successful for years or are just starting out, planning for life is represented by a pyramid of four key stages to align with your goals.:

1. *Income*—with a focus on wages, fixed expenses, and budgeting

2. *Savings*—with a focus on accumulation of funds for unexpected expenses, charitable giving, and for retirement

3. *Protection*—with a focus on assets and obligations such as beneficiaries, debts, and final expenses

4. *Investing*—with a focus on growth to supplement retirement distributions

Each one builds upon and supports the other from a solid foundation.

While planning is unique to each individual, the big question we all need to ask ourselves is, "Does our planning include our retirement and death?" If not, why not? It's not a question to think morbidly about, but to think more clearly about regarding our financial future.

As you plan for life, it would be wise to include a trusted counselor. Just like businesses hire a chief financial officer, a leader needs to consider their own personal advisor. A financial consultant becomes responsible for your personal information and helps you to make informed decisions about your financial future.

### Tips for Finding a Trusted Advisor

- Are they sensitive to your concerns and provide personal options?

- Do they follow up questions with prompt and accurate information?

- Are they able to provide you a personal needs survey questionnaire?

- Are they able to tailor important recommendations to fit your budget?

- Do they care about the pyramid order of planning in your discussions?

- Are they willing to familiarize you with the companies they represent?

- Are they willing to meet with both you and your spouse or loved ones?

- Do you feel they are working from the advantage of their time or yours?

- Do they display an overall appearance of character and professionalism?

*Be careful of this statement:*
*"This is the best option, but you probably can't afford it."*

# Budgets

*Live according to your income.*

~Aulus Persius Flaccus

**W**HEN WE VISIT A DOCTOR FOR A PHYSICAL, they will begin to poke, prod, and press various places on our body while asking, "Does this hurt?" "How about this?" If the response is from pain, two things have happened. Either the doctor pushed too hard, or, more likely, there is something wrong, and more tests are needed. This is similar to when we are challenged to hear about money. Some cry out in discomfort and criticize the message because it either pushed too hard, or something is wrong. The difference with money is this: You and I are responsible for the final diagnosis and the prescribed action steps.

Statistics point out that 80 percent of divorced people indicate that money issues played a primary role. The number of credit cards from the top four credit-card companies reached 679 million in 2018. Projections for 2022 are close to 1.2 billion. Of those individuals with active credit cards, only 40 percent of them are paid in full each month. And, if paid in full, chances are that 28 percent more merchandise was purchased with the card than there would have been with using only cash. It's no wonder the average person spends more money than they make each year.

No doubt there remains a cancer of materialism that continues to reach epidemic proportions in many cultures. John Steinbeck has pointed out that if he wanted to destroy a nation, he would give its people too much and, as a result, have them on their knees, miserable, greedy, and sick. Here is one business owner's philosophy regarding personal credit: "If you ask for credit, and I do not give it to you, you get mad. If I give you credit and you do not pay, I get mad. It is better for you to be mad."

The following quotes and thoughts from other leaders convey

timeless lessons about money. Robert Kiyosaki reminds us that it is not how much money someone makes, but how much they keep, and how hard it works for them. Probably the most challenging thought is from James Moffat: "A man's treatment of money is the most decisive test of his character—how he makes it and how he spends it." And the best definition of money I have ever read: "Money is a universal provider for everything but happiness, and a passport to everywhere but heaven."

The most fundamental tool to help realize these truths, for any family or business, is a budget. A budget is the simplest way to access your current financial situation, define your financial goals, develop a plan, and adjust that plan as time goes on. The basic question to ask is, "Am I controlling my money, or is it controlling me?" A budget is in the first line of self-disciplines to aligning individual planning and goals. Ask yourself these questions about your money situation.

- ❑ Am I living within my means?
- ❑ Do I set aside money each month for savings?
- ❑ Do I have an emergency fund?
- ❑ Am I comfortable with my current cash flow?

### Things to Consider

Don't own things you do not use regularly or do not use at all. Don't purchase and own things just because you can.

*Money is a terrible master, but an excellent servant.*

–P.T. BARNUM

All currency in the United States is stamped with the motto, "In God We Trust." Whenever money is exchanged, there is a small but ever-present reminder that the foundation of life is not money.

# Savings

*Do not save what is left after spending,*
*but spend what is left after saving.*

~Warren Buffett

STANDARDS OF LIVING TAKE MANY FORMS and affect the ability to save. Regardless of where we are in life, it is never too early or too late to begin saving. Making an effort to save and building a personal savings account—even if it's a smaller monthly amount than initially preferred—is significant.

Important things to save for include emergency needs, retirement, and those realized "next opportunities" to reach personal goals. Learn to save for continuing education, equipment needs, and transitioning to a different job or place to live. The concept behind saving is to pay yourself first. Putting aside a certain percentage of your income monthly for the future is key. But how important is saving in your life plan? What are you saving for? To whom would you turn if you fell on hard times? A layoff, illness, or major expense can be an unexpected result of circumstances we do not control. Many people have resorted to receiving help from family and friends. But more people are opting *not* to burden those close to them, and have no one to turn to in time of need.

Saving money and keeping it saved doesn't happen by accident. It takes a disciplined plan that aligns with your goals. Saving is merely an extension of ourselves. Why? Our saving is formed from our time, our abilities, and our efforts. Two questions need to be resolved in deciding to save: "What will I have to give up?" and "What will it cost me?" There are only two kinds of people who seek instant gratification: babies and thieves. By deciding not to save, we will always wonder where the money went. A line in a country song reminds us, "Too much month at the end of the money."

How important is saving to you? If you are already saving, how important is it to you to gradually increase that amount? Consider some basic, risk-free, guaranteed interest savings strategies, in addition to a regular savings and a minimum-balance checking account.

*Certificates of deposit* are one-month to ten-year time deposits to realize some additional interest. Penalties apply for early withdrawal. Rather than establish just one CD with one amount, practice "laddering." You start with more than one CD, altering months and times. This allows for varying due dates and renewal dates, providing more flexibility and options.

*IRAs and Roth IRAs* are specific to retirement or supplement existing retirement plans. Both provide for withdrawals beginning at age 59½. Regular IRAs allow for tax benefits immediately, with taxable withdrawals. Roth IRAs allow for tax-free withdrawals later. A fixed rate, flexible contribution annuity is also an option. It has a set number of years for a surrender period penalty, as well as a 10 percent government penalty for withdrawal prior to age 59½. It's important to consult a planning advisor to determine which strategies are best for you. As a leader, you owe it to yourself, your family, and your ability to earn a living, to take control of your savings.

*An investment in knowledge pays the best interest.*

~Benjamin Franklin

## A Lot to Consider

- How much money could you set aside for savings?
- Do you desire to give more to a church or charity?
- Do you have more than one strategy for saving?
- Do you feel good about the amount you are saving?
- Do you have an emergency fund?
- Do you have a plan to retire or supplement your retirement?

*Saving is a very fine thing if your parents did it for you.*

~Sir Winston Churchill

# Life Insurance

*A man who dies without adequate life insurance should*
*have to come back and see the mess he created.*

~WILL ROGERS

THE MORTALITY RATE IS 100 PERCENT. But, no one expects to die too soon. Each year the death of a leader impacts families and businesses with their hopes for the future. And those relying only on the employee benefit of life insurance discover the plan does not go with them into layoffs and retirement. There is a time when age and health issues make life insurance too expensive...or current medical concerns prevent the issuance of a policy.

The need for life insurance is not temporary. The fundamental question becomes, Have you arranged for the forgiveness of all debts, as well as for a funeral? While the national average for the minimal cost of a funeral is said to be between seven and ten thousand dollars, it is often much higher. It's good to check where you live when considering benefit amounts. And it's easier than you think to overlook vehicles, small personal loans, and second mortgage debts.

The Life Insurance and Market Research group (LIMRA) has noted that seven out of ten families with children under age 18 would have trouble paying bills within two months of a primary wage earner's death. While you cannot put a value on a human life, following the 9/11 attacks, the Victims Compensation Fund valued the future earnings potential of victims at 16 times their income.

Life insurance should not be emphasized and sold as an investment product. It must be offered as a commitment for a leader's peace of mind about the final expenses needed, and the future well-being of those they lead. Money does not offset emotional loss, but it does help reduce the economic loss incurred by those left behind.

> *Every time you send a check to a life insurance company*
> *you make a bet with them. Don't worry, one day you'll win.*
>
> ~NITYA PRAKASH

Life insurance is available as a term product. The most basic and most affordable term coverage is for just that—a specific term. The most common are ten, twenty, or thirty years. At that time, the coverage can be allowed to terminate. It can also be converted to a permanent plan. The term plan itself is also guaranteed renewable, but at significantly higher premiums based on your age at the time. Term is considered most beneficial during those "high debt" years represented by higher mortgages and education costs.

Permanent plans do not expire. In addition to some cash value options, they can even be paid up at certain ages, with continued benefit coverage. Depending on the type of permanent plan and options, you may be able to use cash values to eventually cover premiums, as with a universal plan. Or you may have the option of investing in stocks, bonds, or the money market with a variable plan. The benefits from life insurance are tax free to beneficiaries, but may be included as a part of an estate for tax purposes. The interest in life insurance products with investment options may be taxable.

## Considerations

Personal life insurance should be transparent and simple, but not impulsive.

Business succession life insurance provides funding for effective buy/sell agreements. Life insurance protects accumulated wealth from taxes. Life insurance benefits are determined by net worth, standards of living, and income.

> *Every sale has five basic obstacles:*
> *no need, no money, no hurry, no desire, no trust.*
>
> ~ZIG ZIGLAR

A cautionary sales question:
*How much life insurance would you buy if you knew
you would die tomorrow?*

# Investing

DON'T APPROACH INVESTING LIKE A LOTTERY or slot machine. When thinking of investing, think retirement, not get-rich-quick schemes. For new and veteran investors alike, straightforward and transparent investments are always best. Complexity is not a key component to superior product performance in planning to invest. If you don't understand it, don't put your life savings into it. A good rule of thumb is to invest with the same comfort that you would buy a house. Be content to own it in any market and for the long term. If asked why, you do not need a multiple-word essay answer; it should be a quick and simple response. Don't try to justify yourself for what others may see as a questionable decision.

Investing is usually geared toward answering two questions: "Do I have money to retire with?" and "How long will the money last?" Addressing these concerns with a trusted advisor, along with a plan for the future, can provide peace of mind. For many, a comfortable retirement plan will depend on including mutual funds and variable annuities, in addition to employer retirement plans. For others, it could include purchasing gold or investing directly in the market with individual stocks or bonds.

Remember, the greater potential for gain generally means greater potential for loss. Any risk taken versus any return realized depends on where you are with your overall savings plan, goals, and the additional time required to invest. Here's the good news: Risk comes from *not* knowing what you are doing. Be informed. You need to evaluate your level of comfort in the product you are considering by asking your advisor questions. And then ask again before taking on additional risk in an attempt to achieve greater potential for gains.

When planning retirement investments, do not overlook the projected benefits of Social Security and the cost of Medicare health benefits. Investing does not require being extremely smart, but it does require homework and discipline.

> *Rule Number 1: Never lose money.*
> *Rule Number 2: Don't forget Rule Number 1.*
>
> ~WARREN BUFFETT

Here is a little basic investor education. Mutual funds are professionally managed. Fund managers receive money from a pool of investors, like you and me, and choose the various securities (stock, bonds, etc.) to invest in and monitor in order to help generate the greatest returns. Variable annuities are also professionally managed. Variable annuities allow you to choose from a selection of investments to build a balanced portfolio, or select from a single group or range of "allocated funds" (stocks, bonds, treasuries) in which to invest and have monitored. Along with the potential for returns, both mutual funds and variable annuities have management fees. The key to investing is to stay invested, rather than move in and out of the market. According to the National Bureau of Economic Research and the Federal Reserve, for over 72 years the up markets have lasted longer than the down markets and have more than made up for declines.

Life expectancy in the United States is 78.7 years.
The United Nations estimates global life expectancy at 72.6 years.

Work with an attorney to establish wills and trusts.
When was the last time you reviewed your plan?

Will Social Security and company retirement plans be enough?
It's impossible to predict an up market—it's always possible to miss it.

*The most important investment you can make is in yourself and others.*

# Giving

*It's not how much we give, but how much love we put into giving.*

~MOTHER TERESA

A BUSINESSMAN GAVE AN EXPENSIVE GIFT to a person he wanted to honor. The person insisted, "This gift is too great a gift for me to receive." To which the businessman replied, "But it's not too great a gift for me to give."

The idea of giving financially flows from stewardship. Stewardship is the responsibility we all have for planning and managing resources under our care, such as the environment, health and hygiene, and our finances.

Being intentional about goals, and adopting a lifestyle of making good budget and spending decisions, needs to include the local church, missions, and nonprofit community opportunities. A significant aspect of our financial stewardship is not just about giving money away. It's using a portion of our money for the benefit of others This is not out of obligation but out of a desire of the heart...to experience the joy our generosity brings in blessing others.

Charitable organizations and nonprofit societies are established around specific causes and commonality of the group. Donations are used toward more directly benefiting specific causes. Most often, donations are solicited through random mailings and phone calls.

Our churches are God's established institutions for living out His Word and changing our lives, as well as the lives of many others. It's the church that baptizes us, marries us, and buries us—all the while bringing us to faith and maturity in Christ. The budget of the church is established from those members and guests providing donations in order to pay the pastor, pay the bills, and support certain missionaries. In short, it's keeping the local church functional.

Culture teaches us that we own our money. The Bible teaches that God owns everything. The principle followed is that we are given 100 percent, keeping 90 percent for ourselves and giving back 10 percent to the church and kingdom causes. This practice is a test of faith and an outward commitment to the importance we place on the role of the church.

In Scripture, the idea of 10 percent as a statement of God's ownership of all things became viewed as a religious tax that fulfilled an obligation to the church. The real purpose, however, is meant to embrace using a portion of earnings for the ministry of the church. If we give out of strict obligation or do so begrudgingly, the point has been missed. The Christian view of giving a portion of our money is to use it in ways that glorify God.

Does the Bible, a book that is thousands of years old, really offer any relevancy and guiding principles when it comes to money? Approximately 500 verses deal with prayer. An additional 500 verses deal with faith. Sixteen of the 88 parables and over 2,000 verses deal with money and possessions. In the parable of the talents, we learn the expectation of making wise choices with the money entrusted to us. The Bible does not command poverty, nor does it teach that being obedient or having enough faith will make you wealthy. Yet, virtually every word of Scripture affects how we plan for life. The accountability we have in all that is earned, saved, and invested is to hold the view that it is all entrusted to us by God.

*Don't just think, do.*

~Horace

- Giving intentionally is as important to a planning strategy as anything.
- Giving should be more about a joyful pattern and habit.
- Can you identify a personal deterrent for giving proportionately?
- Are you giving to help build individual and corporate value in others?

- Can you list the top three organizations you do—or could—donate to?
- Is the church you are affiliated with at the top of that list?

# 49

# Tyranny of the Urgent

*Don't let the urgent take the place of the important in your life...*
*when you and I were putting out the fires of the urgent,*
*the important was again left in a holding pattern.*

~CHARLES HUMMEL

"THERE ARE JUST NOT ENOUGH HOURS IN THE DAY to get everything done," said Carl Jenkins as he talked to his executive assistant. "My desk is stacked with papers and unanswered letters. When I opened my e-mails this morning, there were 70 of them, not counting the Spam e-mails. I have a committee meeting in an hour. I have a luncheon with our supplier at noon, and two team group meetings this afternoon. I think I'm going crazy. Everywhere I turn, urgency is crying for attention."

Urgency sometimes screams for immediate attention and drowns out the quiet voice of the important. A fellow employee or a subordinate may seek you out for a pressing decision. Your boss may be expecting a written report on strategic planning. Which comes first? Which is more important? How do we decide priorities?

It begins by putting a value on the issue or decision we're facing. It doesn't matter if it is a choice between two issues or twenty-two issues. Some issues will rise to the surface as an issue of great significance and with long-reaching consequences. The decision might be called profound, momentous, crucial, or of high worth. It's a no-brainer to determine if it's more important to spend time on the boss's report or reading an article in *Time* magazine on earthworms. Hello.

But what if there are two important issues or decisions we're facing? The value system still applies. One of the two decisions will rise above the other because it's of greater worth or "super importance."

Let's say you're in the middle of a very important conference with your CEO and the entire board of directors for your company. All of a sudden, the door opens, and it's your secretary.

"Please forgive me for interrupting, Mr. Jenkins, but I just got a call from the highway patrol. Your wife has been seriously injured in an accident and is being rushed to the hospital." Do you stay, or do you leave? The most important issue puts on hold the lesser important because of its value.

*Do you want to clean up the urgent mess you're facing?*
*Start applying value.*

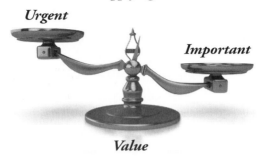

*The important task rarely must be done today, or even this week...But the urgent task calls for instant action...The momentary appeal of these tasks seems irresistible and important, and they devour our energy. But in the light of time's perspective, their deceptive prominence fades; with a sense of loss we recall the vital tasks we pushed aside. We realize we've become slaves to the tyranny of the urgent.*

~Charles Hummel

# 50

# Self-Discipline

*Self-discipline is a character trait that provides the willpower
to do what you should do...whether you like it or not,
or whether you feel like it or not.*

~R.E. PHILLIPS

SUCCESS IN ANY ENDEAVOR does not happen without the energy and work of self-discipline. Do you think it's possible to become an Olympic athlete overnight without workouts and training? Or do you think people will follow you as a leader if you don't have a vision, goals, and the determination to accomplish them? What is your track record for starting and completing tasks?

*Sooner or later all thinking and planning has to degenerate to work.*

~PETER DRUCKER

Would you consider yourself a disciplined person? Are you organized? Are you punctual? Do you have goals? Can you control your thoughts and emotions? Are you clear thinking in a time of crisis? Do you attempt to plan your day? Are you easily sidetracked from tasks? Is it hard for you to retain focus? Can you delay instant gratification for a long-term achievement? Can you tolerate discomfort? Can you resist temptation? Do you have the fortitude to put on your big boy pants or big girl pants and do what you should be doing even if its not fun or likable? Being self-disciplined has a lot to do with simply growing up.

*"How can I become self-controlled or self-disciplined?"* Well, let's start with a question: Do you really want to be self-controlled and self-disciplined? If you do...you will. And if you don't want to be controlled, you won't. It starts by identifying the areas in your life where you're out of control or lack discipline. You won't change that behavior until you're

simply tired of living that way. When you're finally tired of it, then set some goals you would like to accomplish. Make a list of educational goals, financial goals, health-related goals, family goals, recreational goals, business goals, social goals, personal goals, and spiritual goals.

*"Is there some kind of magic in writing down goals that helps you accomplish them?"* Yes, but your goals need to be SMART: **S**pecific, **M**easurable, **A**ttainable, **R**elevant, and **T**ime-bound. A number of years ago, one of my goals was to read 20 books in a year. It met the requirements of being SMART. Within six months, a shocking thing happened: I had reached that goal. Over the years, I continued to raise the goal, and now I read from 80 to 100-plus books a year. Set small goals at first, and then increase them.

Learn to do things you don't like to do. Over the years, I have traveled quite a bit, which includes trips to 30 countries around the world. Wherever I stay—whether it's in a hotel, motel, or someone's home—I always make the bed. You might ask, "Why? Don't they have maids that will make the bed?" Yes, they do, but I make the bed because I don't like making beds. "If you don't like making beds, then why do you do it?" Because I want to be ready to deal with harder issues. I want to stay in "fighting trim." If I can't learn to do "small things" in life that I don't like to do, how will I ever be able to deal with large things I don't like to do?

Discipline is that quality that allows a person to do what needs to be done regardless of the circumstances. Do you need to learn self-discipline? Try beginning with something small that you don't like to do. It will get you started. How about cleaning up your desk, your file cabinet, your closet, or your garage?

> *Self-discipline begins with the mastery of your thoughts.*
> *If you don't control what you think, you can't control what you do.*
> *Simply, self-discipline enables you to think first and act afterward.*
>
> –Napoleon Hill

# Burnout

*Burnout is slang for an inner tiredness, a fatigue of our soul.*

~Mike Yaconelli

ARE YOU A LEADER HEADED TOWARD BURNOUT? The tendency for us as leaders is to work consistently harder and longer and with a growing independence from others. This may be a sign of coping with the inner fight to give up. A decrease in social interactions, along with too many unanticipated and unplanned negative experiences, is often associated with burnout.

*Burnout*, a term first used in the 1970s by psychologist Herbert Freudenberger, may just have been a new label for an old phenomenon. *Burnout* became the word to describe a serious state of exhaustion affecting our physical, intellectual, emotional, and spiritual health.

Authors Schaufeli, Muslach, and Martek point out that burnout is experienced more often with individuals who are highly motivated, working long periods of time, and serving in emotionally demanding jobs. Sound familiar? The seriousness of burnout involves feelings that aspects of the home, work, or the community are out of control—and may even be growing increasingly less meaningful. Are you finding any of these important aspects of your life having less importance and value? Does the feeling of being constantly drained and tired describe you?

Those in every occupation and duty—from emergency first responders to parents raising children—can experience disheartenment, anxiety, and thoughts of quitting that accompany burnout. Passionate, committed, and well-intentioned leaders and followers alike can become deeply disillusioned. Driving too hard and experiencing the effects of sleep deprivation lead to feelings of continual exhaustion and the overall inability to cope.

According to one study, 50 percent of the work force spends more than 12 hours a day at their jobs. As Coach John Wooden has stated, "Don't let yesterday take up too much of today."

Additional symptoms of burnout include blaming others for your personal lack of character, avoiding group social invitations, and turning to thrill-seeking behaviors like drinking, gambling, drugs, and abuse of sex. The effects of burnout on leaders have a most definite impact on our creativity, memory, and problem-solving abilities.

*Burnout is the experience of long-term exhaustion and diminished interest.*

Have you experienced repeated bouts with tension, anxiety, irritability, and anger? Taking time to reverse symptoms of burnout leads to better relationships, overall fulfillment in areas of responsibility, genuine contentment with others, and an inner or spiritual peace of mind. Are these goals you desire? As leaders, we have the task of setting the overall example for others to address burnout by taking the necessary steps to overcome it when it is evident.

*Burnout is the result of too much energy output and not enough energy self-invested.*

~MELISSA STEGINUS

### Additional Identifiers of Burnout

Unclear goals, decreased satisfaction with efforts, self-doubt, withdrawn followers, increased workload pressure, lack of support, negative thoughts, less sympathy, emotional hurts, easily provoked irritations, not enough time, and a continual frustration with inabilities.

*Burnout happens when you try to avoid being human for too long.*

~MICHAEL GUNGOR

### Helpful Tips to Overcoming Burnout

Take indicators seriously, seek professional help as needed, take a vacation or mini retreat, read a book, revisit a hobby or start a new one, attend a one-day conference, listen to a motivational speaker on topics of interest, delegate some responsibilities, learn to say no to some new things.

*Life is not about winning, but finishing well.*

# Holmes & Rahe Stress Test

*The greatest weapon against stress is our ability to choose
one thought over another.*

~WILLIAM JAMES

PSYCHIATRISTS THOMAS HOLMES AND RICHARD RAHE had the belief that stress leads to illness. Take a few moments and gauge where you are with regard to stress in your life. Each life event was given a score. If you have experienced the life event within the last 12 months, write down the score number under the section titled *Your Score,* then total your score at the bottom. As a personal note: When I was in the middle of my master's program, my score was 420. It was then I realized I needed to make some changes.

| Life Event | Value | Your Score |
|---|---|---|
| Death of a spouse | 100 | |
| Divorce | 73 | |
| Marital separation | 65 | |
| Detention in jail | 63 | |
| Death of close family member | 63 | |
| Major personal injury or illness | 53 | |
| Marriage | 50 | |
| Being fired from work | 47 | |
| Retirement from work | 47 | |
| Marital reconciliation | 45 | |
| Major change in health or family behavior | 44 | |
| Pregnancy | 40 | |

| | |
|---|---|
| Sexual difficulties | 39 |
| Gaining a new family member | 39 |
| Major business readjustment/reorganization | 39 |
| Major change in financial status/better or worse | 38 |
| Death of close friend | 37 |
| Changing to different line of work | 36 |
| Major change in arguments with spouse | 35 |
| Mortgage greater than $10,000 | 31 |
| Foreclosure on mortgage or loan | 30 |
| Major change in work responsibilities | 29 |
| Son or daughter leaving home | 29 |
| Trouble with in-laws | 29 |
| Outstanding personal achievement | 28 |
| Wife begins or ceases work | 26 |
| Beginning or ending school | 26 |
| Major change in living conditions | 25 |
| Revision of personal habits | 24 |
| Troubles with boss | 23 |
| Change in work hours / conditions | 20 |
| Change in residence | 20 |
| Changing to a new school | 20 |
| Change in recreation—more / less | 19 |
| Change in church activities | 19 |
| Change in social activities | 18 |
| Mortgage or loan under $10,000 | 17 |
| Change in sleeping habits | 16 |
| Change in family get-togethers | 15 |
| Change in eating habits | 15 |
| Vacation | 13 |
| Christmas | 12 |
| Minor violations of the law | 11 |

YOUR TOTAL LIFE CHANGE
OR TOTAL STRESS LEVEL SCORE_____

Scores of    0-149      A healthy state of being with normal stress

Scores of    150-199    37% likeliness of encountering illness in near future

Scores of    200-299    50% likeliness of encountering illness in near future

Scores of    300 Plus    80% likeliness of encountering illness in near future

# 53

# Self-Control

*In reading the lives of great men, I found that
the first victory they won was over themselves.*

~HARRY S. TRUMAN

BY AGE 16, GEORGE WASHINGTON had copied by hand 110 rules that exemplified good behavior. His first rule: "Every action done in company ought to be with some sign of respect to those that are present." His one hundred tenth rule: "Labor to keep alive in your breast that little spark of celestial fire called conscience." All of his rules could be summed up as a desire to persistently practice self-control.

Far too many leaders are using their position, skills, and influence to attain a lifestyle that is built around personal comforts and conveniences. The needs of others hardly matter to them. The self-control of character, attitude, emotions, and actions are essential to leadership.

Self-control is not a compulsive pursuit of flaws that can somehow be reduced in moderation. Self-control has everything to do with controlling impulsive desires and regulating what we say and do. As it has been said, "Hold tight rein over thoughts, temper, and tongue."

A self-controlled leader is someone who manages behavior, pursues honorable goals, and lives up to certain standards. Why? Because a self-controlled leader understands—to some manner or degree—that they have asked their followers to place their futures in the leader's hands. A self-controlled leader knows that followers don't want to give control of their lives over to someone who can't control their own. A disciplined leader understands that self-control is needed in order to achieve some measure of respect...through the fulfillment of responsibilities in the home, at work, and in the community. Uncontrolled living only leads to frustration and dissatisfaction.

*Those who can command themselves can command others.*

~WILLIAM HAZLITT

In the midst of activity, pursuits, or personal gain, it's important to ask the following question: "Whose life is being enhanced?" If the answer is "Mine" alone, then it would be wise to do a reassessment. I need to reconsider my values in light of all of my responsibilities to those who follow me and depend upon me.

In what areas would you possibly compromise on your self-control? Which areas and circumstances of life are most challenging to your personal emotions and impulses? Is it money, health concerns, man-woman relationships, or time management? Does it occur from a feeling of excitement, boredom, low energy, or increased stress? Does it lead to anger, drinking, gambling, or being a workaholic? Is there an area where you need to work on self-control?

*The journey of a thousand miles begins with one step...watch your step.*

~THOMAS MANSON

Much of the difficulty with self-control is driven by a need for a temporary gratification that lacks any lasting result. The world says, "Live as you please, have what you want, and don't let anyone tell you that you can't." The Judeo-Christian philosophy is one of self-denial, self-restraint, and self-control. Do you have a standard for self-control? If not, might I suggest the example of self-control found in the life of Jesus Christ. I have personally found it to be the most exciting, most challenging, and most satisfying example to follow.

*By consistent self-discipline and self-control you can*
*develop the greatest of character.*

~GRENVILLE KLEISER

### Developing Self-Control

- Name an area in which you desire more self-control.
- State a principle or standard that relates to any needs to be reinforced.

- Identify a way to respond in that specific area with self-control.

- Note one result in which you can recognize success in that area.

# 54

# Vision—Part I

*The presence of vision is one of the most accurate
means of determining if a person is a leader
or merely filling a position of leadership.*

ONE OF THE BIGGEST PROBLEMS WE FACE today is a lack of leadership...and the biggest problem with leadership is finding men and women of character and vision.

It has been said that vision is a mental model of a future state or the creation of something that did not exist before.

- A vision can be a worthy challenge.
- A vision can be appropriate for organizational needs and values.
- A vision might include a set of standards for excellence.
- A vision gives clarification to a particular direction.
- A vision needs to be easy to understand and cause interest.
- A vision attracts people, creates enthusiasm, and inspires commitment.

As a leader, you are responsible for creating vision or carrying out someone else's vision, regardless if it is a large vision (for the entire organization), a medium vision (for a particular department), or a small vision (for a team or group). Wise King Solomon said, "Where there is no vision, the people perish" (Proverbs 29:18 KJV). George Barna makes a strong statement when he says, "No vision equals no leadership."

Now the question arises, Is every leader a visionary? Of course, the answer is no. You've probably worked for a leader who was not a visionary.

They might have even had a difficult time agreeing with or carrying out someone else's vision.

## One Man's Vision

*I will build a motor car for the great multitude...*
*The horse will have disappeared from our highways,*
*the automobile will be taken for granted.*

~HENRY FORD

*A great leader's courage to fulfill his vision*
*comes from passion, not position.*

~JOHN C. MAXWELL

Listed below are some of the characteristics of a visionary. See how many you identify with. Don't feel bad if being a visionary is not your thing. Visionaries rely on faithful people who join with them in carrying out their vision and direction. When two people ride a horse, usually only one has the reins and turns the horse.

|  |  |  |
|---|---|---|
| ❑ A listener | ❑ Decisive | ❑ Persistent |
| ❑ Accepts change | ❑ Idealist | ❑ Practical |
| ❑ Bold | ❑ Imaginative | ❑ Resolute |
| ❑ Charismatic | ❑ Inspires people | ❑ Responsible |
| ❑ Collaborative | ❑ Open minded | ❑ Restless |
| ❑ Conviction | ❑ Opinionated | ❑ Risk taker |
| ❑ Courageous | ❑ Optimistic | ❑ Task oriented |
| ❑ Creates hope | ❑ Passionate | ❑ Thick skinned |

*If God would grant us the vision, the word sacrifice would disappear from our lips and thoughts; we would hate the things that seem now so dear to us; our lives would suddenly be too short, we would despise time-robbing distractions and charge the enemy with all our energies in the name of Christ.*

~NATE SAINT

# Vision—Part II

*A leader's role is to raise people's aspirations for what they can become,*
*and to release their energies so they will try and get there.*

–David Gergen

CHAZOWN (KHAW-ZONE) IS THE HEBREW WORD for vision. It is described as a combination of core values, giftedness, and experience that come together so that dreams and purpose become clear. Vision is designated as being primarily about who we can become, what we are capable of, and what our potential is. Vision is said to be more than identifying what to move away from—it's identifying something possible to move toward. Rosabeth Moss Kanter said it this way; "A vision is not just a picture of what could be, it is an appeal to our better selves, a call to become something more."

The *Harvard Business Review* identifies two principles of vision for a leader to personally identify with: "core ideology" and an "envisioned future." Core ideology represents our central values, plus their primary purpose. These are the essential and enduring principles, and the main reasons you and I have identified for leading and influencing others. In other words, core ideology is what we have determined to hold onto, even if they are or become a competitive disadvantage. An envisioned future is our ability as leaders to identify those bold stretches of ideas and goals, an accompanying description of what it would take, and what it would mean to achieve them. It answers the question, "If we do a good job, what will happen?"

As leaders, our core vision should be a picture of a need being passionately met. A need that is so important it's embedded in our heart. It's a burden on our spirit knowing that we are wired to meet that need.

Steve Jobs suggests, "If you are working on something exciting that you really care about, you don't have to be pushed. The vision pulls you."

Vision must be deeply felt. Vision must be routinely shared. Vision must inspire others. Vision must unify the group. Do you have that kind of vision? Gary Brown noted, "Without vision, we simply project ideas to follow blindly. We become inflexible and resort to long-range planning management. Vision planning is about prioritization."

Is your vision more than a slogan? Does it have a real effect on decision-making and the pulse of your organization? If you've identified a clear, inspirational, long-term desired purpose to be sought, you can then create a vision statement. Vision statements are designed to clearly communicate what it is you are working to achieve in a way that others can remember.

The Pointman Leadership Institute is a professional training group focused on leadership development. Here is their vision statement: "To transform cultures by creating and supporting inspirational, trustworthy leaders."

Aubrey Malphurs and Gordon E. Penfold offer us a personal vision style audit. It's a series of questions that help determine if we are "vision catchers" or "vision casters." Both represent can-do leaders. If we identify as a vision catcher, we are among those who catch a vision by visiting another organization and seeing the vision personally. Vision catchers take hold of the vision and make it a reality. If we identify as a vision caster, we're the type of leader who creates a vision by seeing it in our mind. Our focus is primarily on initiating our own concepts. There is a third style known as a vision cutter. A vision cutter is always mentioning something contrasting to what has been introduced. They will always have an excuse why something will not work, or why it's a bad idea. A vision cutter is not a devil's advocate. In common parlance, the devil's advocate will take a position they do not necessarily agree with for the purpose of debate and exploring the thought further. A vision cutter is just a very negative person. Are you a vision catcher, vision caster, or vision cutter?

# Vision—Part III

*If you are working on something exciting that you really care about, you don't have to be pushed. The vision pulls you.*

~Steve Jobs

**D**O YOU HAVE A VISION THAT DRIVES the organization or institution you lead? As a leader, are you pursuing a unique and compelling foresight for existing? Many leaders are more likely to be focused on reaching financial goals and production targets, while maintaining a rather high profile. A 2014 *Harvard Business Review* study revealed that 70 percent of employees do not understand their company's purpose and strategy.

Author Aubrey Malphurs shares these basic reminders of what vision is not: Vision is not an unrealistic expectation of "too much, too soon." Vision is not about "selling" others on the needed changes. Neither is vision about having to start with a completely blank canvas. It's not even about having to define a completely new sense of direction. He points out that vision is real, credible, timely, and attainable. Vision fosters a can-do environment to help accomplish more together. As a leader it is not necessary to have a concrete plan of what the end looks like. It is more about embracing the process of what a group is to go through to get there. Peter Senge states: "A shared vision is not an idea…it is rather, a force in people's hearts…at its simplest level, a shared vision is the answer to the question 'What do we want to create?'"

Warren Bennis has identified three essentials of leadership: *Develop a vision*—with objectives and goals that are not mystical and require hard work to accomplish. *Communicate the vision*—using repetitive means and redundant methods. *Retain the vision*—with a focus on using a variety of persistent reminders that allow for regular feedback.

A vision lays out the most important primary goals for the organization. A vision is a picture of where things need to be in the near future, with a level of excitement and motivation to do it. A vision is meant to inspire and give direction internally to followers and externally to customers or clients. A vision identifies core values and answers the question, What do we do that aligns with these values in anticipation of the organization's future success? A vision is geared toward seeing a future outcome before it's realized, thus providing a hungry ambition, and justifies a long-term commitment to succeed. I have personally found that vision requires a strong sense of enduring values, a passionate concern for others, and a commitment to stewardship and fiscal responsibility.

Consider these statements about vision from the instruction provided by Pointman Leadership Institute:

- Vision describes a desirable condition of the organization in the not too distant future.
- Vision describes the actions and quality of behavior that provide the desired results.
- Vision illustrates ways followers will achieve results and sets a professional standard.
- Vision sets a bold goal that inspires others to a noble, meaningful purpose or cause.
- Vision is a blueprint to ensure the teamwork needed to achieve the desired goals.
- Vision challenges individuals beyond comfort zones to higher levels of performance.
- Vision is the ability to convert your passion into action consistent with your core values.

As leaders, the ideas for vision come from imagining what the future could be and then working toward that distant goal and purpose. What future goals do you see?

*The greatest danger for most of us is not that our aim*
*is too high and we miss it, but that it is too low and we reach it.*

~MICHELANGELO

# Goofing Off

*I have seen slower people than I am and more deliberate…and even quieter, and more listless, and lazier people than I am. But they were dead.*

~MARK TWAIN

WHEN I WAS IN COLLEGE, I HAD A PART-TIME JOB working for Sears in the stockroom. It was located down in the basement. Next to the stockroom was a snack area that serviced Sears's customers. Employees would also use the snack area when they took morning and afternoon breaks.

It didn't take me long to realize there are two types of employees. The first are those employees that show up *at* work. The second are those employees that show up *to* work. This was especially noticed during the morning and afternoon break times.

The employees that show up *at* work would say, "It's ten o'clock, I'm going to take a break." They would slowly meander to the restroom. When that was accomplished, they would slowly meander out the double swinging doors to the snack area. They would place their order and then wait to pick it up. Then they would slowly find a table and sit down. It was at that point they would look at their watch and then begin their 15-minute break—which really was like 20 minutes. Then they would slowly get up and meander back into the stockroom and start putting in some work time. This same procedure was repeated during the afternoon break period. Those employees didn't show up *to* work. It was more like goofing off.

One time I attended a meeting where the speaker was introduced, and then she asked for some help to pass out notepaper. Then she asked for some help to pass pencils to anyone who did not have a pen to write with. There were about 400 people in attendance. The whole process took about ten minutes before she started speaking. Then she said, "If I would have been organized, I would have already had the paper and pencil on your chair when you arrived. Since I wasn't organized, I wasted about ten minutes of your time. Now multiply that by 400 people in the room. That's 4,000 minutes of unproductive time. Now divide the 4,000 minutes by 60 minutes in an hour. That means I just wasted 66 man-hours of time." To say the least, she certainly drove home a point.

One of the biggest frustrations that fellow employees deal with is watching other fellow employees or team members goof off while others are striving for excellence. What discourages them even more is when those in leadership do not address goofing off at work, whether it is planned goofing off like long breaks, or unplanned goofing off because of disorganization, poor skills, and an unawareness of the bigger picture.

When was the last time you did an inventory of your organization with a focus on finding areas of goofing off or disorganization? Or do you know it's there, and you're just turning a blind eye to it? You may want to be liked and not be seen as a mean monster cracking the whip.

Stop for a minute and think about it. If you're aware of employees goofing off, the odds are that the other employees are aware of it too. Your not dealing with the issue is conveying a message to everyone who works for you. Your message is, "It's okay to goof off under my leadership."

*Responsibility is the thing people dread most of all.*
*Yet it is the one thing in the world that develops us,*
*gives our manhood or womanhood fiber.*

~Frank Crane

### *Did you have some fiber today?*

# Leadership Skills

*Consider the questions below in relation to your leadership needs and responsibilities. Place a check in the box if it applies to you or it is an area you need to work on.*

❑ **Do you have a readiness for responsibility?**

- ○ *Leadership is a potent combination of strategy and character. But if you must be without one, be without the strategy.* —Norman Schwarzkopf

- ○ *I believe that every right implies a responsibility; every opportunity, an obligation; every possession, a duty.*—John D. Rockefeller

❑ **Are you constantly thinking about vision and plans?**

- ○ *Do not go where the path may lead, go instead where there is no path and leave a trail.*—Ralph Waldo Emerson

- ○ *Vision is the art of seeing things invisible.*—Jonathan Swift

❑ **Do you anticipate needs and see the big picture?**

- ○ *The future has several names. For the weak, it is the impossible. For the fainthearted, it is the unknown. For the thoughtful and valiant, it is ideal.*—Victor Hugo

- ○ *The future belongs to people who see possibilities before they become obvious.*—Ted Levitt

❑ **Is anyone following you? If not, why not?**

- ○ *The final test of a leader is that he leaves behind him in other men the conviction and the will to carry on.*—Walter Lippmann

- ○ *To be a leader, you have to make people want to follow you, and nobody wants to follow someone who doesn't know where he's going.*—Joe Namath

❑ **Would people be willing to go into battle with you?**

○ *Leadership is a matter of having people look at you and gain confidence, seeing how you react. If you're in control, they're in control.*—Tom Landry

❑ **Do you display a positive or negative attitude?**

○ *The longer I live the more convinced I become that life is 10 percent what happens to us and 90 percent how we respond to it.*—Charles R. Swindoll

○ *Where there is an open mind, there will always be a frontier.*—Charles Kettering

❑ **Are you loyal to the authority over you?**

○ *When leaders throughout an organization take an active, genuine interest in the people they manage, when they invest real time to understand employees at a fundamental level, they create a climate for greater morale, loyalty, and, yes, growth.*—Patrick Lencioni

❑ **Do you enjoy oversight of important projects?**

○ *If you want favor with both God and man, and a reputation for good judgment and common sense, then trust the Lord completely; don't ever trust yourself. In everything you do, put God first, and he will direct you and crown your efforts with success.*—Proverbs 3:5-6

❑ **Do you sense when others are unclear in their thinking?**

○ *Common sense is the knack of seeing things as they are, and doing things as they ought to be done.*—Calvin E. Stowe

○ *Before it can be solved, a problem must be clearly stated and defined.*—William Feather

# Priorities

*Unless we come apart and rest awhile, we may just come apart.*

~Vance Havner

THERE ARE TIMES AND OCCASIONS for giving ourselves over to nonstop work activity. This was something I had to prepare for often as a police detective and jail commander. I also had to confront the fact that leaders can lose the ability to find time to relax. I witnessed firsthand how in a fast-paced, success-oriented society, allowing life to get out of balance can have devastating consequences. In fact, studies have shown that the more imbalance we have, the more our emotional intelligence and decision-making abilities plummet.

Rest, recreation, and relationships can be neglected, and self-destructive tendencies can go unchecked. How many of us really think life is underwhelming and we desire to be much busier? Do you really wish days could be more filled because life is just not demanding enough? Regardless of gender, race, religion, or socioeconomic status, leaders and followers alike would like to find ways to live life with more balance.

Brian Tracy notes, "You perform better when your thoughts, feelings, emotions, goals, and values are in balance." Jim Schleckser points out, "There are seven elements in seeking balance in life—health, family, social, financial, business, civic, and spiritual." These would seem to indicate that balance is not as simple as negotiating between work and home. Life itself is in constant motion with all kinds of priorities, obligations, relationships, and interests that compete for our time and attention. Each of us desire to be independently sought without the guilt and feeling that "I should be doing something else."

Balance has been described as "how we do the things we have to do, and the things we want to do, without changing the number of hours in a day." Yet, to prioritize all this is easier said than done. First, to prioritize doesn't mean to designate some things as more important than others as much as it honestly addresses those things that can wait. And yes, it's fair to realize that age and experience do affect the way people prioritize. Second, prioritization is not to procrastinate or abuse time. It's important to sense that the urgency of time is fragile and short. Balance is accepting a healthy perspective of the reality that there is much to do.

Instead of competing priorities against each other, shouldn't we learn to collaborate them? Seek balance as a habit in the long term, not just occasionally. Treat balance not as an infinite goal, but a process and continual way of living. The truth about balance is that it needs to reappear over and over again. And, while both accomplishments and failures are part of practicing a balanced life, those leaders who commit to the process of balance develop good relationships, are more personally sustainable for the long term, experience greater fulfillment, and are generally more content.

I have personally learned to take Sunday as a day for finding balance. It's a church day, a family day, an opportunity to do something good for others day. It's a time to rest from regular weekly labors, receive spiritual encouragement, and invest in family activities. And if not a Sunday, as often was the case in the law enforcement profession, then a day that did fit the schedule. Regardless of the day, it should lead to rest, perspective, and the reordering of life. I believe Zig Ziglar summed it up best: "I believe that being successful means having a balance of success stories across the many areas of life."

### Are You Seeking a Balanced Life?

Do you have a sense of overcommitment? Do you feel the need to make time for everyone and everything? Do you have interests and activities you never find the time to do? Do you know someone who wants to take a walk with you? Do you need 30 minutes to just stop and do some thinking? Take time and schedule it.

# Effective Communication

*The two words information and communication are often used interchangeably, but they signify quite different things. Information is giving out; communication is getting through.*

~Sydney J. Harris

COMMUNICATION IS A PROCESS where information is passed from one individual to another by using language, signs, symbols, and behavior. To be effective in sharing your thoughts with another person, it's good to remember eight simple concepts:

**#1—Language is not always precise.** The same word when spoken can be perceived and mean different things to different people. The sender may say *father,* meaning their own natural parent. The receiver might envision a priest. The word *freedom* to a teenager might mean no longer under the control of their parents. To a mother with two toddlers, it might mean having someone watch the children while they get some needed rest.

**#2—The sender is more responsible for the message.** If the sender picks up that the receiver of a message is confused, resistant, or downright hostile, it would be important to stop and ask, "What did you hear me saying?" If the receiver plays back a different message, the sender needs to clarify the misunderstanding.

**#3—Verbal communication must match nonverbal communication.** If the sender says, "I love you" while clinching their teeth, yelling, and shaking their fist at the same time, the message will be contradictory and will not be believed.

**#4—Positive and negative statements must not be given together.** "Hey, Bill, it's great to see you...putting on a little weight, I see."

What do you think Bill will remember? You have just lost the power of a positive thought.

**#5—In confronting, attack the issue and not the person.** Use "I" words rather than "you" words that can come across as aggressive: "You never clean up the dirty dishes!" "I" words are assertive but do not attack: "I would appreciate it if you would clean up the dirty dishes when you are through."

**#6—Clear up unspoken expectations.** Most people do not carry a crystal ball around with them to discover expectations that were never expressed. Silence is the most dangerous thing in a marriage or while working alongside other people. The Amish technique of "shunning" (treating another person as if they did not exist and shutting down all communication) destroys relationships.

**#7—Pick the right time for heavy discussions.** Most family arguments take place half an hour before dinner or half an hour before leaving for school or work when everyone is tired or highly stressed. Heavy discussions that occur after 9:00 p.m. have a tendency to go downhill. People are tired and want to sleep and know that the matter will probably not be resolved. The discussion will begin with a negative attitude to begin with. Pick a better time.

**#8—Speak the truth in love.** Tone down the hostility. Turn up the kindness.

*Everyone enjoys giving good advice, and how wonderful it is to be able to say the right thing at the right time.*

~Proverbs 15:23

*Timely advice is as lovely as gold apples in a silver basket.*

~Proverbs 25:11

*A gentle answer turns away wrath, but harsh words cause quarrels.*

~Proverbs 15:1

# Meeting Template

*We are going to continue having these meetings, every day,*
*until I find out why no work is getting done.*

~Richard Moran

**Purpose of Meeting:** _____

❑ One-on-One Meeting     ❑ Two or More People

❑ Resolving Problems     ❑ Teaching and Training

❑ Informational Meeting     ❑ Questions and Answers

❑ Decision-Making     ❑ Celebration/Party

❑ Unity and Staff Morale     ❑ Negotiation Meeting

❑ Impromptu Meeting     ❑ Brainstorming / Ideas

Other: _____

Date:_____ Time: _____

Location: _____

**Who NEEDS to Attend the Meeting:** _____

❑ Those Offering Information     ❑ Those Offering Expertise

❑ Those Offering Advice     ❑ Those Offering Action

• Start meetings on time even if some people are late. Don't reinforce their tardiness by waiting. It shows disrespect for those on time. Speak privately to chronic offenders of time.

- Avoid "from here to eternity" marathon, nonproductive meetings.

  ✓ Write a better agenda and stick to it.

  ✓ Place important and "heavier" issues as number one on the agenda. Don't put them off toward the end of the agenda, or the meeting will drag on.

  ✓ Set an actual timer with a bell to limit discussions. That's fun.

  ✓ Don't let one individual monopolize the discussion.

  ✓ Ask those in attendance to suggest solutions rather than talking about problems forever—anyone can do that.

  *Either meet or work. You can't do both at the same time.*
  ~Peter Drucker

- Try holding a "stand up" meeting. No one is allowed to sit down. This is guaranteed to speed the meeting up. I even heard in early American history that when it came to some jury trials that the members of the jury were not allowed to go to the bathroom until a decision was reached. I don't think you can get away with that one.

- Multiply the hourly salary of everyone by the time you think it will take to hold a meeting. It will help you to calculate the importance of how much time and expense you will allocate for a meeting. Is it really worth the time spent? It has been said that executives who spend a lot of time in meetings are probably disorganized. How much time are you spending in meetings?

- Don't approve of or allow unruly and disruptive members to distract the meeting. Name-calling, sarcastic put-downs, and wisecracks are attempts to control. It is important for people to have freedom to express themselves, but not at the expense of another. It's okay to challenge ideas—just not the person. In essentials—*unity*. In nonessentials—*liberty*. In everything—*love*.

- As much as possible, attempt to have "circle" meetings where all those in attendance can see the face of everyone in attendance. It increases understanding—and control.

*I've searched all the parks in all the cities*
*and found no statues of Committees.*

~GILBERT K. CHESTERTON

# Total Communication

*Communicate downward to subordinates with at least the same
care and attention as you communicate upward to superiors.*

~L.B. Belker

HAVE YOU EVER RECEIVED AN E-MAIL where the content has disturbed you? You're not quite sure if the sender is joking or is serious. You can't tell if they are angry, sarcastic, or just trying to be funny.

Part of the problem lies in the fact that the e-mail does not contain tone of voice. Tone helps us understand the sender's feelings and attitude toward the communication. Another factor is nonverbal behavior. It's also not in the e-mail. We can't read facial expressions and body language. You need to have all three—words, tone, and body language—to have effective communication.

In the 1960s and '70s, Albert Mehrabian did his famous work on nonverbal communication. His research discovered that the content of words only made up 7 percent of the communication message. Tone of voice made up 38 percent, and body language made up 55 percent. He found that the more congruent or matching...the more believable and understandable the message was.

For example: If I said to you with a smiling face and laughing manner, "The building is on fire"...and then sat down and poured a cup of coffee, would that be clear and effective communication? I think most people would be confused. What if I said, "The building is on fire," and my face showed shock and fear, and I was yelling at the top of my voice. Then I ran out of the room, leaving you there. Would that be effective communication? I doubt you would sit there and pour a cup of coffee.

How effective are you in your communication? Do your words, tone, and body language all match? Or are you a leader who says that you care about and trust your followers while speaking with an angry and hostile tone and emphasizing your care with inappropriate body language?

Have your family, friends, or fellow workers ever mentioned that you have a negative tone? This week make a concerted effort to become aware of your words, tone, and body language. Benjamin Franklin said, "Speak little, do much."

On a scale of 1 to 10, how congruent is
your communication message?

Dismal  1  2  3  4  5  6  7  8  9  10  Pretty good

*The most important thing in communication
is hearing what isn't said.*

~PETER DRUCKER

# Service

*Leadership must embody servanthood, for without it
leadership will become the embodiment of our selfish agendas.*

~CRAIG D. LOUNSBROUGH

FOR GOOD REASON, JOHN MAXWELL HAS STATED, "The first step of leadership is servanthood." Simon Sinek, in his book *Leaders Eat Last*, points out that United States Marine Corps officers eat last. He describes how this is done purposely because there is a realized cost to leadership: "They put their own interests aside. Leaders would sooner sacrifice what is theirs, to save what is ours. And, they would never sacrifice what is ours, to save what is theirs." The privilege of leadership comes at the self-sacrifice of personal interests for the good of those impacted by the immediate sphere of our influence.

There is a natural tendency in all of us to look toward self-interests first. We tend to elevate ourselves and our status. We need to guard against overlooking our service with an inflated ego, arrogance, and pride. Some leaders use their skills to attain a lifestyle that is built around their own comfort and convenience. Unfortunately, leadership is often understood in terms of assertiveness, ambition, and material success alone. Have you ever been caught up in the awards and accolades in a need to proclaim personal success? The servility of leadership is born out of an obligation to do the minimum necessary according to what others see. It's an attitude of pride and answers the question, "What's in it for me?" However, leadership by these values will take an organization into circumstances no one wants to experience. Robert Greenleaf suggests, "The first and most important choice a leader makes is the choice to serve. Without which one's capacity to lead is severely limited." Whether leadership is viewed as arriving by following a political agenda, or by a more legitimate means through earned privilege, there is a danger of being self-centered rather than follower centered.

*If leadership serves only the leader, it will fail.*

~Sheila Murray Bethel

Servant leadership is about making a choice of the heart to help, prepare, and invest in others. James Konzes and Barry Posner confirm that "leadership is not an affair of the head. Leadership is an affair of the heart." The heart of servant leadership is one of obedience. It's an attitude of humility and asks, "What's in it for them?"

Servant leaders will look at the needs of others along with, or ahead of, their own needs. And, leaders should not make the mistake of excusing disobedience toward the purpose of servant leadership by pointing to their poor upbringing, personal history, or culture. If that's the case, then you and I have the ability to change it. J. Carla Nortcult reminds us, "The goal of many leaders is to get people to think more highly of the leader. The goal of a great leader is to help people think more highly of themselves."

In the midst of all leadership pursuits, we need to ask ourselves, "Whose life is being enhanced by what I do?" If the only answer is, "Mine," it seems obvious the needs of others matter little. As a leader, what is your posture toward those you have influence over? Do you see others as beneficiaries of your leadership? Are you committed to investing in another person's time, future, and sense of self-worth? Followers have value. Followers need to be recognized. Is there anything that captivates our attention and interest more than those followers who are depending on us?

*Just as the Son of man came not to be waited on but to serve, and to give His life as a ransom for many.*

~Matthew 20:28

*Do all the good you can and make as little fuss about it as possible.*

~Charles Dickens

# Command Presence

*Your first and foremost job as a leader is to take charge of your own energy and then help to orchestrate the energy of those around you.*

~Peter Drucker

WHAT IN THE WORLD IS COMMAND PRESENCE? Some have commented: "It's a mysterious inner quality of leadership that some people have. I don't know how to describe it, but I know it when I see it." Let's drive down a little and attempt to describe it.

Command presence involves quite a bit of nonverbal communication. There is something about the way the individual carries himself or herself. They seem to move with purpose and direction. They walk and stand tall with their shoulders held back and do not stoop, slouch, shrug, or have rounded shoulders. They seem to have a sense of professionalism and military bearing that projects authority, strong influence, and the ability to control. There is something about them that creates a sense of energy.

When they shake your hand, you can feel their confidence. Their handshake is not weak or limp like a dead fish. It's firm and strong, but not overpowering like you've been crushed in a vise. As they shake your hand, you're aware of a very slight lean forward, as they look you directly in the eye.

When they speak, their voice is not whispery, wimpy, or whining. It seems to have a quality of clarity, control, and calmness. Their speech is candid and remarkably open, matter-of-fact, and honest. Their eyes are focused and alert and seem to grasp you and the entire room. It's like they make a quick assessment of the situation and people.

*An eye can threaten like a loaded and leveled gun,*
*or it can insult like hissing or kicking; or, in its altered mood,*
*by beams of kindness, it can make the heart dance for joy.*

~RALPH WALDO EMERSON

Some have suggested that a person with charisma (the ability to attract and inspire individuals) is the same as having command presence. This is not always true. There are a number of inspirational people that would not be good leaders.

The question arises, Which comes first? Does command presence drive motivation and actions, or do actions create what is called command presence? You see, it's possible to walk and stand tall and look people in the eye. You can fake all the nonverbal behaviors of command presence. The question is, Can you deliver? Would people really want to follow you?

Individuals with command presence are people with high energy, enthusiasm, and optimism. They have the ability to process information rapidly and drive down quickly to the key issues at hand. They are action and results oriented. They are highly motivated to accomplish goals. Their energy and results orientation is attractive. Their ability to accomplish goals and tasks often sets them apart from others. People seem to rally around those who are moving forward with excitement and purpose.

Being a person of command presence is more than having a firm handshake. It has to do with integrity, character, and intent. Command presence is created in the crucible of honest work, perseverance, and self-discipline. Command presence has a great deal to do with trust. People do not want to follow people they do not trust.

Are you worried about having command presence? Worry more about your motivation, inspiration, and actions. Command presence is not something you're born with. It's something you earn and grow into by diligence, faithfulness, and commitment.

*There's a difference between interest and commitment.*
*When you're interested in doing something you only*
*do it when it's convenient. When you're committed to*
*something, you accept no excuses; only results.*

~KENNETH BLANCHARD

# Setting Goals

*What you get by achieving your goals is not as*
*important as what you become by achieving your goals.*

~Zig Ziglar

ALL SUCCESSFUL LEADERS HAVE GOALS. No one can truly get anywhere unless they know where they want to go, identify what they want to do, and realize who they want to become. From education, to a healthy diet, to a financially secure retirement, every person's life depends on the process of choosing which goals to pursue.

As leaders we set goals for ourselves, our families, and for our careers. Here are four important reasons for establishing goals:

1. Goals help to overcome any tendency to procrastinate.

2. Goals tend to foster positive behavior rather than negative behavior.

3. Goals become plans of action that provide direction and see us through to realized accomplishments.

4. Goals become our personalized road maps that set the direction and provide a means of evaluating progress.

Goals, whether mentally envisioned or written out specifically, require a clear, measurable, and actionable target. A clear goal is a goal that is specific, realistic, and attainable.

*Set a goal that commands your thoughts,*
*liberties, your energy, and inspires your hopes.*

~Andrew Carnegie

*Goals are pure fantasy unless you a have a specific plan to achieve them.*

~STEVEN COVEY

An actionable goal is a goal that has deadlines, time frames, and is eventually realized. Actionable goals identify the standards of behavior and actions by which to perform and complete the task.

*Discipline is the bridge between goals and accomplishment.*

~JIM ROHN

If goals are not clear, measurable, and actionable, they will actually have a negative effect and impact on all our efforts. Unclear goals are easily manipulated and demotivate us.

If the goal is to write a book, it comes into clear focus by choosing specific topics and setting a desired completion date. It becomes measurable by the habit of regularly scheduled writings to complete each week and seeking edits and reviews. And it becomes actionable when the rules and guidelines of ethical publishing are followed—regardless if the book is actually published or not.

Commitments to goals are as important as the goals themselves. What are the demands and the degree of difficulty? A good question to ask is, "Am I willing to accept the sacrifices required to achieve this goal?"

*You are never too old to set a new goal or to dream a new dream.*

~C.S. LEWIS

Take a few moments and write down some of your goals:

❑ Business Goal

_____

❑ Financial Goal

_____

❑ Educational Goal

_____

❑ Family Goal

_____

❑ Health Goal

_____

❑ Social Goal

_____

❑ Spiritual Goal

_____

# Decision-Making

*I believe that we are solely responsible for our choices,*
*and we have to accept the consequences of every deed,*
*word, and thought throughout our lifetime.*

–ELISABETH KUBLER-ROSS

SOME DECISIONS ARE AS SIMPLE AS, "Would you like vanilla or chocolate ice cream?" The decisions become a little more confusing when you add 31 flavors of ice cream to choose from. Making decisions can have long-term, life-changing results, like getting married, selecting a career, or doing something criminal like murdering a person.

The process of decision-making is often complex because there are many variables. They include beliefs, customs, facts, biases, values, emotions, objectives, alternatives, an introvert or extrovert temperament, preferences, positive or negative outcomes, wishful thinking, and peer pressure or group think.

Decision-making can be slowed because of a negative attitude. It can be hampered by fears of failure or rejection by other people. Decision-making comes to a standstill by having too much information to consider. Facts and details are important, but they can create a short circuit because of too much data. It causes what's known as "analysis paralysis."

The first task is to identify, clarify, and simplify the decision to be made. The second task is to identify who is to make the decision: an individual or a group of people. Next, is it a major decision or a minor decision? And it's important to know the timing in which the decision has to be made. Does the decision need to be made immediately, or is there extended time to consider various options or to acquire additional information?

Here's a fun way to decide an issue between two possible choices:

Decision A or Decision B. Hand your friend a coin, and make Decision A *heads* and Decision B *tails.* Then have your friend flip the coin. The next step is very important. Make a commitment to yourself that you will call either *heads* or *tails* while the coin is in the air and before it hits the ground.

The choice you make while the coin is in the air is the choice you really desire. It's the one you really want to happen. The mix of all the information you have, your emotions, and your intuition (instinctive belief) will cause you to either call *heads* or *tails.* It's a cool way in helping people to decide. Try it...you'll like it.

*If you want favor with both God and man, and a reputation*
*for good judgment and common sense, then trust the Lord*
*completely; don't ever trust yourself.*
*In everything you do, put God first, and he will direct you*
*and crown your efforts with success.*

~Proverbs 3:5-6

# Decision-Making Template

*Describe the decision to be made.*

_____

_____

*What area of concern does the decision involve?*

❏ Routine ❏ Strategic ❏ Financial ❏ Operational
❏ Relational ❏ Emergency ❏ Other _____

*What type of decision is it?*

❏ Irreversible ❏ Reversible ❏ Experimental ❏ Trial and Error
❏ Cautious ❏ Delayed ❏ Conditional ❏ Made in Stages

*What is the time frame for the decision?*

❏ Crisis ❏ Urgent ❏ Week ❏ Month ❏ 6 Months ❏ Year

*What is the effect of the decision?*

❏ A decision for the short term ❏ A decision for the long term

*Who needs to make this decision?*

❏ An individual—Name _____

❏ A group or committee—How many people? _____
Do the members have the necessary education, past experience, wisdom? Are they creative?—Do they have good street smarts?—Do they have an understanding of the big picture?—Can they keep confidences?—Do they represent

a wide range of thinking?—Are they open to risk taking?—Are they decision makers?

### *What is the desired outcome from the group or committee?*

❏ A unified consensus or general agreement from the group?

❏ A supporting agreement where some members disagree but will not put road blocks or hinder the decision?

❏ A 50-50 decision from the group where the leader makes the final choice?

### *Apply SWOT to the decision:*

**S**trengths of the decision
**W**eakness of the decision
**O**pportunities created by the decision
**T**hreats created by the decision

* * * * * * * * * * * * * * * * * * * *

*The percentages of mistakes in quick decisions is no greater than in long, drawn-out vacillations, and the effect of decisiveness itself "makes things go" and creates confidence.* -Anne O'Hare McCormick

* * * * * * * * * * * * * * * * * * * * * * *

## Two Models of Decision-Making

### Model A

- Identify the problem.
- Gather and clarify information.
- Analyze the facts and data.
- Weigh options and alternatives.
- Consider consequences.
- Choose the best alternative.
- Assign responsibility.
- Evaluate and follow up.
- Modify if necessary.

### Model B

- Start with mission and values.
- Clarify the situation.
- Review policies.
- Choose procedures.
- Review legislation.
- Consider risk appetite.
- Evaluate possible outcomes.
- Make the decision.
- Review results.
- Make adjustments.

# Leadership Competence

*Consider the questions below in relation to your leadership needs and responsibilities. Place a check in the box if it applies to you or it is an area you need to work on.*

❑ **Are you willing to make the tough decisions?**

- ○ *Gather all the facts possible and then make your decision on what you think is right, as opposed to what you think is wrong. Don't try to guess what others will think, whether they will praise or deride you. And always remember that at least some of your decisions will probably be wrong. Do this and you always will sleep well at night.*—Douglas MacArthur

❑ **Do you make things simple for those following you?**

- ○ *Everything should be made as simple as possible, but not simpler.*—Albert Einstein

- ○ *Simple is nice.*—R.E. Phillips

❑ **Do you deal in a positive way to interruptions in your schedule?**

- ○ *Interruptions are God's unexpected opportunities.*

- ○ *My whole life I have been complaining that my work was constantly interrupted, until I discovered that my interruptions were my work.*—Henri Nouwen

❑ **Can you hang on when the going gets very tough?**

- ○ *This acrostic informs us how to GROW through difficulties:*

**G**o

   **R**ight

      **O**n

         **W**orking

❑ **Can you handle criticism and rejection?**

- ○ *If you can find a path with no obstacles, it probably doesn't lead anywhere.*—Frank A. Clark

- ○ *When you are getting kicked from the rear, it means you're in front.*—Fulton J. Sheen

❑ **Can you pass on the hard issues and the bad news to your followers?**

- ○ *I like long walks, especially when they are taken by people who annoy me.*—Fred Allen

- ○ *Difficulties are God's errands; and when we are sent upon them, we should esteem it a proof of God's confidence—as a compliment from him.*—Henry Ward Beecher

❑ **Can you work with a team of very different individuals?**

- ○ *People are the way they are. Get past the need to try to change them, past the need to judge or condemn, and look for the value they offer. Sometimes that value is deeply hidden, and when you find it you've found a real treasure, something few people take the time to uncover. In every difficult person you encounter, make a point to look past the difficult part and focus your attention on the person part.*—Ralph Marston

❑ **Do you seek practical ways of helping others?**

- ○ *In about the same degree as you are helpful, you will be happy.*—Karl Reiland

- ○ *When I was young, I admired clever people. Now that I am old, I admire kind people.*—Abraham Joshua Heschel

❑ **Have you supervised and guided others toward success?**

- ○ *The most important single ingredient in the formula of success is knowing how to get along with people.*—Theodore Roosevelt

- ○ *The key to success is setting aside eight hours a day for work and eight hours for sleep and making sure they're not the same hours.*

# The Bottleneck

*The commander in the field is always right and the rear echelon is wrong, unless proved otherwise. In my experience, the people closest to the problems are often in the best position to see the solutions. The key here is to empower and not be the bottleneck.*

~Colin Powell

A BOTTLENECK REFERS TO SOMETHING smaller than the whole. A good example is an hourglass. It's large at the top, small in the middle, and large at the bottom. A large amount of sand is attempting to reach the bottom of the glass but is slowed down or impeded by a small or narrow opening.

When it comes to a bottle, the larger portion is at the bottom and the smaller opening is at the top. The smaller opening is located in the neck of the bottle—hence we call it the bottleneck. When you attempt to pour out what's in the bottle, the process is hampered. A point of congestion occurs in the neck of the bottle.

A bottleneck could occur in the areas of equipment or materials. A broken part in a large machine could slow or stop all progress.

A lack of a supply of bumpers could retard the production of automobiles.

A bottleneck in a process or an activity can retard momentum and create unnecessary and frustrating activities. A classic example of this is the creation of endless reams of paperwork and "red tape" that employees hate with a passion. This often occurs when bureaucracy grows, procedures become complicated, and the most listened-to people are the accountants and bookkeepers.

A bottleneck in the management of people or the decision-making process can be a major hindrance in forward movement in any business or organization. It can also be a problem in the smooth running of a family.

Peter Drucker suggests, "In most organizations, the bottleneck is at the top of the bottle." The "buck" stops with the leader. A major part of any leader's job is to process information, identify problems, seek solutions, and make decisions.

For years I used to keep a drawing of a bottle next to my desk. The bottle was loaded with people who were trying to get out of a bottle. Seated in the neck of the bottle was one person who was blocking the forward movement of the people. It was a reminder to me that every time I slowed down in making a decision, I was slowing down the entire organization. I was hired to make decisions, not to sit there twiddling my thumbs. Where are you sitting today? Are you making the necessary decisions?

## *The Bottleneck*

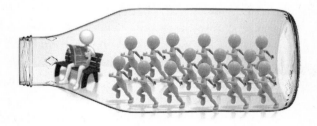

# Persuasiveness

*Leadership is about persuasion, presentation, and people skills.*

~Shiv Khera

GET WHAT YOU CAN WITH WORDS because words are free. But the words of an armed man ring much sweeter." Let's consider that Joe Abercrombie is referring to being "equipped" with the skills that enhance our ability to be convincing. The other option is to simply smile.

Persuasiveness is a key competency of leadership. Truth is foundational to having a direct positive effect. It's based on a leader's motives. If a leader cannot persuade with truth to get support for an idea, agenda, or direction, they need to reconsider what they are trying to accomplish.

It was Aristotle who is credited with identifying and naming the system of writing and speaking to inform and persuade specific audiences. This system is known as "Aristotle's Ingredients of Persuasion." Included are ethos, pathos, logos, and kairos. Let's review these.

Ethos, or body, represents the image of the leader. It considers reputation, credentials, and experience. It causes the recipient to ask, "Why should I attend and listen?" Logos, or head, represents the words and content of the leader's message. It considers the structure, substance, and truth of the message. It causes the recipient to ask, "What evidence am I being provided?" Pathos, or heart, represents the emotion, need, and desire. It considers the individual's beliefs and values. It causes the recipient to ask, "How is this making me feel?" Kairos, or culture, represents the timeliness of the message. It relates to the appropriateness and overall general consensus. It causes the recipient to ask, "Do I support this?"

Persuasive leaders consider each of Aristotle's elements in considering the best interests of both the individual and themselves.

Here are some unpopular techniques of persuasion: playing upon emotional fears and asking for unspecified risks—not sales pitches everyone appreciates. The strategy of reminding people of what their peers and everyone else is doing does not produce good "buy-in" results. Setting an unrealistic sense of urgency and forcing time restraints disregards people's thoughts and decision-making process. Rather, people are persuaded by a purpose and reason why. People are persuaded by someone giving them direction and encouragement to reach their goals. People are persuaded and challenged by the expectation to do what they are capable of.

*If you would persuade, you must appeal to interest rather than intellect.*

~Benjamin Franklin

People are persuaded when their personal needs are met in three distinct areas. *Dependence*—They have confidence in being led toward a significant decision and achievement that gives them peace of mind, money, safety, and ownership. *Independence*—Here the focus is on personal abilities, qualities, and knowledge. This includes communication skills, flexibility, and character. *Interdependence*—This involves an interconnection with a collectively beneficial team of two or more people with the same mutual aims, such as job security, continuing education, and team recognition. Consider the following suggestions:

- Relate the significance of the action to be taken to the purpose and mission.

- Convey the impact of how their contribution enhances the success of the goal.

- Arrange tasks that will challenge others to be part of group accomplishments.

- Explain how individual achievements fit into the overall big picture.

- Provide for others the opportunities to experience and master new skills.

- Acknowledge the benefits and awards for the commitments expected.

> *Being persuasive is really something you learn at an early age.*
> *You'd be amazed how many teenagers get their first car*
> *by talking about a motorcycle.*

# 71

# Loving Leadership

*You will find as you look back upon your life that the moments*
*when you have really lived are the moments when you*
*have done things in the spirit of love.*

~HENRY DRUMMOND

ANCIENT GREEK PHILOSOPHERS HAD FIVE WORDS to describe the word *love*. The first was *storge*, which referred to familial love. It was followed by *philia*—friendly love, *eros*—romantic love, *xenia*—guest love, and *agape*—which spoke of divine love. All of the words expressed depth of feelings that are played out in action:

| | | |
|---|---|---|
| Admiration | Compassion | Enthusiasm |
| Affection | Concern | Kindness |
| Benevolence | Devotion | Unselfishness |

The ability to express love is important not only within our own family but also with fellow workers and in all of our relationships. In the following, rate your ability to express love with your family and others.

1. *This love of which I speak is slow to lose patience.*
   Love doesn't demonstrate irritations or reflect anger or have a quick temper. Love bears ill treatment from others.

2. *Love looks for a way of being constructive.*
   Love is actively creative. Love is able to recognize needs. Love mellows all that would be harsh and austere.

3. *Love is not possessive.*
   Love is not envious. Love does not hold exclusive control where someone is allowed little or no freedom to fulfill himself or herself apart from the other individual.

4. *Love is not anxious to impress.*
   Love does not brag. Love doesn't seek to make an impression or create an image for personal gain. Love does not show itself off.

5. *Love does not cherish inflated ideas of its own importance.*
   Love does not put on airs. Love is not self-centered. Love has the ability to change and to accept change. Love is not on an ego trip.

6. *Love has good manners.*
   Love has respect for others, which results in a set of godly standards. Love does not act unbecomingly or unmannerly. Love is not indecent.

7. *Love does not pursue selfish advantage.*
   Love does not insist on its own way. Love does not have primary concern for personal appetites but concern for the needs of the other person.

8. *Love is not touchy.*
   Love is not easily angered. Love does not take things too personally. Love is thick skinned. Love bears no malice.

9. *Love does not keep account of evil.*
   Love doesn't review wrongs which have been forgiven. Love doesn't dwell on past evil. Love keeps no score of past hurts.

10. *Love does not gloat over the wickedness of other people.*
    Love doesn't compare self with others for self-justification. Love doesn't use others' evil to excuse personal weakness.

11. *Love rejoices when truth prevails.*
    Love is active in fellowship and dedicated to fellow believers. Love is occupied with spiritual objectives. Love rejoices at the victory of truth.

12. *Love knows no limit to its self-control and tolerance.*
    Love has the ability to live with the inconsistencies of others. Love is slow to expose. Love can overlook faults.

13. *Love knows no end to its trust.*
    Love expresses faith in everything. Love believes in the person and the person's worth without question.

14. *Love is always hopeful.*
    Love is not fickle. Love has perfect peace and confidence in the future.

15. *Love has unlimited endurance.*
    Love is able to outlast anything. There is nothing that love cannot face.

# 72

# Forgiveness Is an Attitude

*Forgiveness forces you to grow beyond what you were.*

FORGIVENESS IS NOT OFTEN IDENTIFIED as a character trait of leadership...but it should be. At least it's a positive result of learning and practice. There is no indication, regardless of the level of offense, that forgiveness is not a difficult skill to be developed. Like other character traits, it's not an easy journey. It does not come naturally. It's hard to consider forgiveness if we continue to hold on to pride, jealousy, and hate, and let revengeful feelings get in the way. As someone has said, forgiveness is a great idea, until we personally have to practice it. Why should forgiveness be a significant part of our leadership and character? Besides remembering that others are watching our responses to any conflict, as leaders we also have an obligation to strive to do what is ultimately right.

First, let's be very clear. Forgiveness has nothing to do with being seen as either a winner or loser. Forgiveness is not about tolerating continual offenses or subjecting ourselves to the same painful circumstances. Forgiveness is not about waiting until feeling that someone has earned or deserves it. Forgiveness does not mean we suppress anger or approve of what happened. Neither is forgiveness about forgetting what happened, hiding our grief, or being expected to exonerate an offender.

History and current events remind us all of criminal acts of racism, murder, and terrorism. Many individuals directly and personally are challenged to forgive some of the most horrendous acts directed at those closest to them. While it's challenging for most to imagine how difficult that would be, the challenge is in understanding that forgiveness is more about you and me than the offender. Bosses, coworkers, parents, spouses, children, and neighbors are all going to disappoint us at some level with something said or done. Some may even hurt us deeply.

The truth is that imperfect people follow imperfect leaders. That's you and I. Our disappointment and hurt degenerates into prolonged feelings of anger. Prolonged feelings of anger result in bitterness, resentment, and endless cycles of thoughts of retaliation. This leads to uncontrolled emotions and destruction of our self-worth and health. An unforgiving spirit slowly poisons our very outlook on life. Even to the point of harboring a faulty belief that God somehow holds the same view of us as we do. Do we agree that as grueling as forgiveness is, it is important to our overall leadership?

Forgiveness is an attitude, a voluntary action. Forgiveness is a choice. As Corrie ten Boom noted, "Forgiveness is an act of the will." Learning to accept limitations in ourselves and developing an ability to let go of hate is necessary. Hate destroys our influence and personality. If we harbor hate and obsess about what others have done, we get consumed and often become spiteful people and leaders. Have you felt this kind of hatred? If so, know that forgiveness is central to our emotional and spiritual well-being. How you and I feel about ourselves is going to strongly affect the way we relate to others. Dr. Wrede Vogel shares that a friend of his, who is a pastor and clinical psychologist, noted that a major problem contributing to psychological disorders is tied to a patient's lack of understanding of forgiveness. Do you need to forgive someone?

Yes, forgiveness is risky—because we give up the right to a list of hurts and demands.

Suppose God spoke and said, *"I'll settle the score with them for you. I'll base my judgment upon your perfect marriage, your perfect family, your perfect parenting, your perfect friendship, your perfect career, your perfect leadership, your perfect character—which one should it be?"*

Do we really want God to judge someone on our behalf? Forgiveness has been made possible through Christ's pain and suffering. Remind yourself of this when Satan tries to manipulate your thinking about forgiveness.

# Loneliness

*Uneasy lies the head that wears the crown.*

~Shakespeare

HAVE YOU EVER HAD FEELINGS OF LONELINESS? If you have, you're not alone. Loneliness is a universal malady, as witnessed recently in the United Kingdom. Not long ago, they voted in a Minister of Loneliness to deal with issues inflicting their society. A US News & World Report suggested that 54 percent of people always or sometimes feel lonely.

Another study indicated that as many as one-third of workers say that they have no strong relationships at work. But what about those who are in leadership? Seventy percent of first-time CEOs admit that they deal with loneliness, and 61 percent of longer-term CEOs classify themselves as lonely.

Why does loneliness hit so many leaders? The answer is not complex. The mere fact that they are a leader puts them in a position of separation from the followers. Leaders have to be concerned with the "big picture" of the total organization, while employees tend to focus on their particular job. Leaders have more information and have to sometimes keep more confidences. Employees usually do not have to think about the responsibilities and accountability of:

| | | |
|---|---|---|
| Directing | Guiding | Managing |
| Deciding | Counseling | Encouraging |
| Challenging | Legal issues | Financial oversight |
| Company image | Employee benefits | Governmental problems |
| Board relationships | Conflict management | Company morale |

The leader experiences a type of loneliness when they enter a room and suddenly employee conversations change. The leader cannot share in friendships on the same level as employees—which enhances separation and loneliness.

*You can be loved, respected, successful, appreciated,*
*but still feel like you're swinging the sword alone.*

## Combatting Leadership Loneliness

- Learn not to confide in the wrong people.
- Develop friendships outside of the workplace.
- Do not neglect to get sufficient exercise and rest.
- Spend time reading books and articles on leadership.
- Accept the fact that the leadership role creates some loneliness.
- Develop trusted confidantes outside of your work environment.
- Seek peer support from other leaders who are in similar positions.
- Reach out for some executive coaching or a mentor/mentee relationship.
- Develop an avocation or hobby that expresses your creativity and brings you satisfaction.

- Balance your life in relationship to your spouse, children, recreation, and church.

- Remind yourself of the need for courage to stand alone and make tough decisions.

- Develop your spiritual life through prayer and Bible reading. Ask God to give you wisdom and direction in all of your responsibilities.

> *We expect our leaders to be better than we are...and*
> *they should be—or why are we following them?*
>
> ~PAUL HARVEY

# 74

# Loyalty

*Lack of loyalty is one of the major causes of failure in every walk of life.*

~Napoleon Hill

AS A GENERAL RULE, THERE ARE THREE AREAS of betrayal that receive universal scorn. The first is *adultery* when it breaks a relationship. The second is *treason* when it violates a membership. The third is *idolatry* when it destroys not only a relationship and membership, but also a destiny.

The word *loyalty* carries with it various shades of meaning like allegiance, attachment, and affection. It can mean commitment, constancy, and credibility. It also includes dedication, devotion, and dependability. And we can't leave out faithfulness, support, and obligation.

*Loyalty is not just a word—it's a lifestyle.*

Not only does loyalty have shades of meaning, but it also has many areas where it can be demonstrated. The first loyalty that we learn is to become loyal to our family unit: our father, mother, and siblings. Other areas of loyalty can include:

- Church
- Club
- Community
- Ethnic group
- Fellow veterans

- Friends
- God
- Language
- Nation
- Peers

- Political parties
- Profession
- Religion
- School
- Team

With regard to loyalty, it's an either/or situation. There's no middle ground. You're either loyal or you're not. It's sort of like being pregnant. There's no in between.

Jesus talks about loyalty when He says, "No one can serve two masters. For you will hate one and love the other; you will be devoted to one and despise the other. You cannot serve God and be enslaved to money" (Luke 16:13 NLT). His point is that you have a choice.

The apostle Paul addresses the concept of sowing and reaping when he says,

> *Do not be deceived, God is not mocked [He will not allow Himself to be ridiculed, nor treated with contempt nor allow His precepts to be scornfully set aside]; for whatever a man sows, this and this only is what he will reap. For the one who sows to his flesh [his sinful capacity, his worldliness, his disgraceful impulses] will reap from the flesh ruin and destruction, but the one who sows to the Spirit will from the Spirit reap eternal life* (Galatians 6:7-8 AMP).

When we apply the sowing and reaping concept to loyalty, we realize that by being loyal there will be positive results. Loyalty builds trust between people. On the other side, disloyalty and betrayal destroys relationships.

When soldiers fight on the battlefield, do you think they are focused on saving their country? I'm sure it's somewhere in the back of their mind, but it's not their main focus. Their main focus is to depend upon the loyalty of their fellow soldiers as they try to work together to stay alive. What would happen if there was one disloyal soldier among the group? What do you think will happen in your organization when disloyalty raises its ugly head?

> *We can become great in the eyes of others, but we'll never become successful when we compromise our character and show disloyalty toward friends or teammates. The reverse is also true: No individual or team will become great without loyalty.*
>
> –JOHN WOODEN

# 75

# Disloyalty

*Disloyalty in trusted servants is one of the most disheartening
things that can happen to a public performer.*

~HARRY HOUDINI

D O YOU HAVE A FEW MINUTES TO TALK?" asked Ruddy.
"Sure," said Ethan. "What's up?"

"I've heard the big bosses are talking about the need for loyalty in our company."

"I have too. It's part of a character-building program they've instituted."

"I'm finding it hard to be loyal and respectful to my boss when he makes such stupid decisions. Don't get me wrong, some of his decisions are okay, but he really makes some poor ones."

"Have you talked with him about your concerns?"

"Are you kidding? I don't want to be fired."

"How do you handle the orders and decisions he gives you?" asked Ethan.

"Well, when he gives me several things to do, I pick the ones I agree with, and I tell the members of my team that we will do the good and right decisions. And the poor decisions—we won't put as much energy into them because the boss hasn't really thought them through."

"Ruddy, that's an interesting way of reacting. Did your boss ask you to do anything immoral, unethical, or illegal?"

"No. Of course not. His ideas are just a little crazy."

"It sounds like you are in disagreement with him."

"You've got that right."

"Let me see if I hear you correctly. You disagree with your boss and think his ideas and decisions are silly. He didn't give you any orders to do anything wrong. You haven't talked with him about his ideas. And you're telling those who work for you not to follow his orders. That sounds like you're jealous and can make better decisions...you're disobedient and rebellious...and you are disruptive and spreading discord with those who work for you. Does that sort of sum it up?"

"Well..."

"Ruddy, he's the boss. He does pay your salary...and you disagree with him and want to undercut his leadership. Would you want an employee like you working for you? When you tell your team to not obey all of his orders, you're teaching them to do the same thing when you give them orders. You're teaching them to gripe and complain about you. It sounds like you're struggling with submission to legitimate authority above you."

> *Like charcoal to hot embers and wood to fire, so is a contentious man to kindle strife. The words of a whisper (gossip) are like dainty morsels [to be greedily eaten]...A hot-tempered man stirs up strife, but he who is slow to anger and patient calms disputes.*
>
> ~Proverbs 26:21-22; 15:18 AMP

# 76

# Rekindling Loyalty

*Loyalty is essential to the most basic things that make life livable.*
*Without loyalty there can be no love. Without loyalty there can*
*be no family. Without loyalty there can be no friendship.*
*Without loyalty there can be no commitment to community or*
*country. And without those things, there can be no society.*

~Eric Felton

ETHAN, I'VE BEEN THINKING OVER WHAT YOU SAID when we last met," said Ruddy. "Could I share with you what I've been thinking?"

"Of course," said Ethan. "I've got the time."

"After our talk the other day, I've realized why I have not been successful in my leadership. I now know why people don't follow me. It's because I don't follow the leaders over me. I've not been submissive to their leadership. I know I need to change that."

"That's great insight. It will make a big difference for you. When you're in leadership and have questions or complaints, you don't share your disagreements downward to your followers. It only confuses them and destroys trust. If you have concerns, you need to share them upward to your boss."

"I guess that's where I have a question. How do I share a concern or disagreement with one of his ideas or something he asks me to do that I think is not the best thing?"

"Honesty is always the best policy. First, talk to him in private and not in front of a group. Approach him when he is not super busy or rushed. Respect his time and pressures. Say something like, 'Sir, do I have permission to speak frankly?' When he says yes, then share your concern without attacking him as a person. Deal with the issue or the direction you're asked to follow. Don't just share your concern and disagreement. Share the thinking behind your disagreement, and don't just share problems. Also come with suggested solutions or additional information that will help to clarify your concerns.

"He may agree with you. He may disagree with you. Either way, you need to follow his leadership unless he is asking you to do anything immoral, illegal, or unethical. Relax, and do what he asks you to do. The bottom line is, your leader is ultimately responsible for his decisions."

"I'll have to work at that."

"It might be a little difficult at first, but it will get better. Let me give you an illustration. Have you ever seen a wild stallion running in a pasture? Stallions are beautiful animals to look at. They're strong and free...but their strength is good for nothing until they become broken and can be directed by a bridle. It's only when the stallion obeys the trainer that their great strength can be a benefit to others. Are you ready to take the bit and the bridle and obey the direction of the trainer? Or to use another illustration, think about a powerful locomotive on a train. What is the purpose of a locomotive? Is it to toot the whistle...or is it to pull a load?"

> *Loyalty is something you give regardless of what you get back,*
> *and in giving loyalty, you're getting more loyalty; and out of*
> *loyalty flow other great qualities.*
>
> ~CHARLES JONES

> *Loyalty is what makes us trust, trust is what makes us stay.*
> *Staying is what makes us love, and love is what gives us hope.*
>
> ~GLENN VAN DEKKEN

# 77

# Leadership Aptitude

*Consider the questions below in relation to your leadership needs and responsibilities. Place a check in the box if it applies to you or it is an area you need to work on.*

❑ **Are you willing to risk, grow, and learn?**

- ○ *If we don't change, we don't grow. If we don't grow, we are not living. Growth demands a temporary surrender of security.*—Gail Sheehy

❑ **Do you have a track record for getting things done?**

- ○ *The three great essentials to achieve anything worthwhile are, first, hard work; second, stick-to-itiveness; third, common sense.*—Thomas Edison

- ○ *Achievement comes after hard work, not before. "If people knew how hard I worked to get my mastery, it wouldn't seem so wonderful after all."*—Michelangelo

❑ **Are you willing to work long and hard hours?**

- ○ *Nothing ever comes to one, that is worth having, except as a result of hard work.*—Booker T. Washington

- ○ *Hard work spotlights the character of people: some turn up their sleeves, some turn up their noses, and some don't turn up at all.*—Sam Ewing

❑ **Can you make adjustments when faced with frustration and dead ends?**

- ○ *Expectation feeds frustration. It is an unhealthy attachment to people, things, and outcomes we wish we could control; but don't.*—Steve Maraboli

- ○ *Realize that if you have time to whine and complain about something, then you have the time to do something about it.*—Anthony J. D'Angelo

❑ **Can you deal with all the weird, strange, and annoying people?**

- ○ *We can learn silence from the talkative, patience with the intolerant, and kindness from the mean, yet somehow we don't seem to like those strange people because at times we are them.*—R.E. Phillips

❑ **Can you keep the flame of enthusiasm burning?**

- ○ *Nothing great was ever achieved without enthusiasm.* —Ralph Waldo Emerson

- ○ *Nothing is so contagious as enthusiasm.*—Edward Bulwer-Lytton

❑ **Are you looking for people to mentor?**

- ○ *Leadership by example is not one form of leading—it is likely the only effective form.*

- ○ *It's very important to pick the right mentor who will guide you properly. Very few people get to the top without being taken under the wing of an older person somewhere along the way.*—Jean Paul Lyet

❑ **Are you willing to carry the burden and responsibility of the position?**

- ○ *Not many of you should become teachers, my fellow believers, because you know that we who teach will be judged more strictly.*—James 3:1 NIV

- ○ *Responsibility is the thing people dread most of all. Yet it is the one thing in the world that develops us, gives our manhood or womanhood fiber.*—Frank Crane

❑ **Do you have a natural enthusiasm and enjoyment for leadership?**

    ° *If you can't get enthusiastic about your work, it's time to get alarmed—something is wrong. Compete with yourself; set your teeth and dive into the job of breaking your own record. No one keeps up his enthusiasm automatically. Enthusiasm must be nourished with new actions, new aspirations, new efforts, new vision. It is one's own fault if his enthusiasm is gone; he has failed to feed it. If you want to turn hours into minutes, renew your enthusiasm.*—Papyrus

❑ **Do other people give you affirmation that you have leadership skills?**

    ° *Get someone else to blow your horn and the sound will carry twice as far.*—Will Rogers

# Understanding Stress

*We can easily manage if we will only take, each day,*
*the burden appointed to it. But the load will be too heavy for us*
*if we carry yesterday's burden over again today, and then add*
*the burden of the morrow before we are required to bear it.*

~JOHN NEWTON

WHAT IS STRESS? Stress is a physical, mental, or emotional pressure, tension, or strain. Pressure because it can be caused from an outside source, event, or circumstance. A tension created by imbalance in stretching too far, or a tightening and constricting. Or a strain that leads to overextension or bending toward a painful breaking point.

No one is totally free of stress because there are four types of stress. The first is *too little stress* that leads to dullness, boredom, apathy, and laziness. The second is *healthy stress* that encourages excitement, fun, productivity, and positiveness. The third area of stress is *unproductive stress*. This type of stress leads to overalertness, mental and physical discomfort, increased worry and concern, and unwanted pressure and tension. The final area is *unhealthy stress* that leads to strain, burnout, illness, and death. The first key is to determine which of the four areas is causing the most discomfort.

Stress affects our body in different ways. The key is to become alert to our body's attempt to display early warning signs of stress.

## Emotional Signs

| | | |
|---|---|---|
| Boredom | Detachment | Irritability |
| Confusion | Escape thoughts | Listlessness |
| Depression | Impatience | Nervousness |

## Visceral Signs

| Cold hands | Fainting | Nausea |
| Diarrhea | Heartburn | Sweating |
| Dry mouth | Moist hands | Ulcers |

## Musculoskeletal Signs

| Back pain | Headaches | Stiff neck |
| Fidgeting | Jaw tightening | Tense muscles |
| Grinding teeth | Shaky hands | Tics and twitches |

## Other Signs

| Compulsiveness | Hair twisting | Neglecting family |
| Exhaustion | Low spiritual life | Neglecting friends |
| Fatigue | Nail-biting | Neglecting fun |

❏ Is the stress permanent like the death of a loved one, or situational like the loss of a job? Accept and make peace with what you cannot change. Work on the situational issues and problems that you have control of.

❏ Learn to say "no" to taking on too much work. Get organized to gain extra time. Delegate to release your load. Tackle the biggest problem or issue first. It will be the hardest...and smaller issues will be downhill (or easier) from there.

❏ Learn to turn your troubles over to God. *Dear brothers, is your life full of difficulties and temptations? Then be happy, for when the way is rough, your patience has a chance to grow* —James 1:2-3.

*Stress Cycle*

# Respect

*If you can have some respect for people as they are, you can be
more effective in helping them to become better than they are.*

~John W. Gardner

IN 1947, JACKIE ROBINSON was the first to break the "color barrier"
in major league baseball. History records for us that Robinson endured
excessive bias, racial abuse, and unfairness. Mr. Robinson once remarked
to journalists during an interview, "I'm not concerned with your liking
me or disliking me. All I ask is that you respect me as a human being."
We understand much better now that being rude and inconsiderate is
a trait of selfish people, and it begins at early ages. As Dr. Billy Graham
noted, "Most will tell you a child who is allowed to be disrespectful to
parents will not have true respect for anyone."

Law enforcement officers around the world respond to hundreds
of thousands of calls of criminal misconduct each day involving both
juveniles and adults. They range from harassment complaints to murder investigations. These acts perpetuated on others represent the emotions and intentions of the heart and stem from anger, hate, and jealousy
of another human being. Many of these circumstances result in lifelong
consequences because of choices made in a moment of utter disrespect
for human lives. Do not misunderstand. There are those who need and
deserve justice. But respect also ensures that any punishment provided
fits the crime, and that it's not carried out at the hands of others for personal retribution.

Even those who are ordinarily controlled can, under certain circumstances, respond impulsively and do or say things often regretted later on.
Consider the controversial but relevant issues of abortion and euthana-
sia. Also, do not overlook outward circumstances like the level of poverty,

personal health, or degree of physical disability. Committing suicide is an extreme act revealing a lack of self-respect.

Exercising respect is to act with thoughtfulness and civility. Respect has been identified as a behavior, a value, an attitude, a motive, a duty, and a principle. Whatever the view taken, it means avoiding any violation or interference with someone else's boundary lines or personal space.

Roy T. Bennet points out that "respect seems to be a choice based on human rights, needs, and relationships." Perhaps what we as leaders and followers seek and want more than anything else is mutual respect. It's the ability to look upon someone else—and be looked upon ourselves—with a general understanding for one another with regard to design and purpose. It's a design and purpose first given to each of us by God alone.

When we treat others with respect, it shows we recognize this fundamental value and worth in all individuals. I believe a pursuit of personal character traits and adhering to identifiable foundational principles helps us in providing the level of respect we all seek to be treated with. How are you doing with the respect of others?

## Consider...

- Talking to others the way you would like to be talked to.

- Placing no lesser status on others based on gender, age, race, or position.

- Hearing others out. Evaluate their words and emotions with an open mind.

- Taking time to deliberately acknowledge those who need and deserve your attention.

- Become increasingly aware of your role to protect those weaker and more vulnerable.

*A person is a person no matter how small.*

~Dr. Seuss

# 80

# Crisis Response

*Every little thing counts in a crisis.*

~JAWAHARLAL NEHRU

EVERY LEADER AND ORGANIZATION IS VULNERABLE to a crisis. A critical incident is the event; a crisis is the acute emotional reaction. A critical incident can occur unexpectedly, suddenly, and without warning. It can also be more of a gradual development. It's surprising and less disruptive. Webster's dictionary describes a crisis as "a serious state of things—an unstable condition requiring necessary judgment—a crucial time." Any crisis is a time of trouble, difficulty, or danger for everybody affected. A crisis can stem from a natural disaster, financial blow, technological predicament, or a catastrophic event involving malicious behavior. Each crisis has a far-reaching ripple effect upon individuals, groups, and communities. Every crisis has the potential to change lives and organizations forever.

During a crisis, we are told that 75 percent of people directly affected will be temporarily unfocused in their response. Another 10 to 25 percent will be affected long term. And 10 to 15 percent will be calm and controlled. Leadership needs to be in that 10 to 15 percent. The number of people experiencing these outcomes varies directly with the severity of the exposure—ranging from infrequent symptoms to severe and lasting trauma. Regardless of the crisis, it is an adjustment for everyone. Developing a crisis intervention program is highly recommended.

*In times of crisis, people search for meaning. Meaning is strength. Our survival may depend on seeking and finding it.*

~VIKTOR E. FRANKL

A leader needs to be aware of the thoughts and needs of those impacted by a crisis. These thoughts can range from uncertainty—due to rumors and opinions, to turmoil—created by restlessness and fear, to revenge—due to wanting to harm others. It's recommended to bring together those groups experiencing a crisis within 72 hours for a debriefing. The Mitchel-Everly Critical Incident Stress Management Model (see the Internet) addresses eight phases of adjustment. It's one option that continues to be utilized by most first responders. Please do not overlook the professionals in your community willing to assist.

*In every crisis, doubt, or confusion, take the higher path,*
*the path of compassion, courage, understanding, and love.*

~AMIT RAY

As a leader, others will naturally assume you have the ability to deal with any given critical situation. Let's look at some responses to build confidence and a strong organizational structure.

The following communication tips and policy guide require deliberate interaction, effective coping skills, and increased organizational and community cohesion. It helps to instill pride and promotes relationships in the most difficult of times.

### Communication
*Be confident in your ability to be there.*

**Timely**—A human presence cannot be replaced, even if there's no solution.
**Personal**—The need to convey respect and reassurance is crucial.
**Plain language**—Confirm the worst without unnecessary detail.
**Team**—Show unified strength and care.
**Compassion**—Demeanor is a most valuable resource.

### Crisis Policy Guide

**Principle**—Ensure safety and protect lives.
**Policy**—Maintain order.
**Strategy**—Protect human rights, dignity.
**Tactic**—Provide an effective professional appearance.
**Action**—Document, understand, communicate.

# 81

# Personal Development

*What it lies in our power to do, it lies in our power not to do.*

~Aristotle

PERSONAL DEVELOPMENT DEMANDS that both time and action are necessary for continual improvement. It's the responsibility of leaders to influence others in positive ways. This involves a passion for achieving excellence and effectiveness. It's a process that doesn't happen overnight.

It has been said that time itself is not the problem...but people who use it are. One calendar year is equal to 8,760 hours. If the average night's rest is eight hours, you and I will sleep one-third of our lives. If we live to be 75 years of age, that's 50 years of activity and 25 years of sleep.

There is a depth of insight reflected in the above facts. The desire to become a more significant leader demands that we spend time to gain personal knowledge and experience in leadership. How are we to do this?

Two words come to mind. The first is *priority*. It's a fact or condition regarded as more important than another. Is developing leadership skills an important priority for you or not? The second is *competence*. It's the ability to do something efficiently and proficiently. Do you purposely set aside time to improve your leadership skills through reading leadership books, attending leadership seminars, or consulting with other leaders?

One way to prioritize and gain a feeling of competence for any task or work is to make a to-do list. There is something gratifying about seeing a list accomplished and placing that all-familiar check mark next to those items on the list that are completed. These checklists are a means to identify goals to be fulfilled over a certain period of time. Making a list of priorities shows a more competent leader. In the Bible, God instructed Moses to build the tabernacle according to a specific list (Exodus 25–31).

When Jesus sent out the 12 disciples, He sent them with a specific list of what to take and where to stay (Matthew 10:1-15).

In the book *Excellence in Leadership*, author Frank Goble provides a thought list of certain things to do in a serious pursuit of developing your personal leadership skills. The common denominator you will find in each one is to ask, "When am I going to put this into action?"

### MONDAY
❑ Make plans to attend a leadership seminar.

### TUESDAY
❑ Read a magazine article about leadership.

### WEDNESDAY
❑ Ask for recommendations on leadership books to read.

### THURSDAY
❑ Start a leadership library of books you want to and have read.

### FRIDAY
❑ Display indicators of the quality of leadership you desire.

### Interesting Fact

Almost everyone struggles with getting things done. Studies have shown that 95 percent of people *do not* have written goals. Of the 5 percent who *do* have written goals, they reach 95 percent of their goals. Lists reduce the anxiety of recall and procrastination, plus help people to prioritize and maintain focus. How are you doing?

*Keep in mind that it often does not take much effort to do things, but it does require effort to decide on what needs to be accomplished.*

# Mistakes, Muddles, and Missteps

*A bad leader can take a good staff and destroy it,*
*causing the best employees to flee and*
*the remainder to lose all motivation.*

~Joseph Lalonde

WHY IS THERE A CRYING NEED for good and effective leadership? The answer to the question is not complex...it's quite simple. It's because there is such a high degree of bad and ineffective leadership.

What are the underlying causes of poor and sometimes terrible leadership? History and culture give us our first clues. The majority of human history is littered with kings, tribal leaders, controlling families, dictators, chiefs, monarchs, emperors, commanders, and high priests. They all have a similar thread running through them. The thread is control. They are in charge, and you need to listen to them, obey them, and serve them. They are the boss in no uncertain terms. This is basically autocratic, top-down leadership that wants its way and is usually not friendly to seeking advice, having open communication, and any form of democracy. Certain cultures in our world today have operated in this fashion from the beginning of recorded human history.

Other clues to why poor leadership occurs are:

- No good leadership examples to follow
- Confused value systems
- Poor leadership skills and no formal training
- Good old-fashioned selfishness

Listed below are examples of leadership mistakes, muddles, and missteps. As you begin to read through them, be alert to areas that might be potential pitfalls in your own leadership influence in the lives of others.

- ☐ **Avoiding conflict**—This usually occurs because of fear. You don't want be the bad guy. You want to be seen as a caring, neutral person who is liked by everyone. Sorry, you weren't hired to be liked...you were hired to lead.

- ☐ **Being a boss**—Yes, we know you're in charge. The question is, Are you leading or are you being bossy? If it's not clear what bossy means, let's expand it a little. Bossy includes being dictatorial, domineering, overbearing, overreactive, stubborn, or even tyrannical. Does that help?

- ☐ **Being invisible**—If people don't see you actively involved as a leader, they will begin to question if they're working for a ghost. Where is he or she? What do they do? Who's running this place? Does the boss travel in underground tunnels?

- ☐ **Being too friendly**—It's great to have a winsome, friendly leader. It's great to get to know them personally. However, sometimes it would be nice if they would not take up so much time that I can't get my work done. And if you're too friendly, they may begin to see you as a fellow worker shooting the breeze rather than the leader they have to answer to. Do you talk too much?

- ☐ **Blame shifting**—Don't you just love it when the leader is perfect? They never make a mistake. What a joy it is to have everyone think you're the idiot who messed everything up as the leader blames you. Maybe there's a message here someplace.

> *A leader is one who sees more than others see, who sees farther than others see, and who sees before others see.*
>
> –LeRoy Eims

# I Quit!

*Some 80% of your life is spent working. You want to have
fun at home; why shouldn't you have fun at work?*

~RICHARD BRANSON

HAVE YOU EVER FELT LIKE QUITTING YOUR PRESENT JOB? The Bureau of Labor Statistics suggests that men and women change their jobs 12 times in their lifetime. So much for the question, "What do you want to do when you grow up?"

Some people ask, "How long should I stay at a job?" It all depends what the job is like and the satisfaction you get from it. Below you will see what the average job life is for different age groups.

✓ **For those 25 to 34**—The average time on the job before change is 2.8 years.

✓ **For those 35 to 44**—The average time on the job before change is 4.9 years.

✓ **For those 45 to 54**—The average time on the job before change is 7.6 years.

✓ **For those 55 to 64**—The average time on the job before change is 10.1 years.

Various reasons for wanting to change jobs or careers include:

- Higher pay
- Better benefits
- Career advancement
- Less stress
- Difficult employers
- Change of interest

- Better work/life balance
- Reorganization and layoffs
- Better work schedule
- Lack of recognition
- No training possibilities
- Lack of challenge

I remember Olan Hendrix once saying, "I realized that I stayed one year too long at my last job." That phrase has haunted me for years. Who would want to stay one year too long at any job? Have you been too long at your job?

Listed below are red flags that signal the possible need for a job transition. Check the ones that apply to you:

- ❑ Boredom
- ❑ Watching the clock
- ❑ Daydreaming
- ❑ Searching the Web for jobs
- ❑ Not a fit with other employees
- ❑ Trouble with your boss
- ❑ Your boss is younger than you
- ❑ You're at the top of your game
- ❑ Not challenged anymore
- ❑ Too much routine
- ❑ Other employees drive you crazy
- ❑ Feel bigger than the job
- ❑ No advancement opportunities
- ❑ Inexperience of those you work with
- ❑ Disappointment with the vision
- ❑ Would like to try something new
- ❑ Feel like you're not growing
- ❑ "I don't care anymore" attitude
- ❑ Feel depressed and angry

*"Okay, I admit I'm a little dissatisfied. Now what? It will probably take me two years to get settled and learn a new career."*

"How old will you be in two years if you decide to change careers?"
*"I would be two years older."*
"How old will you be in two years if you stay in the same job?"
*"I would be two years older."*
"Which would you rather be, two years older in your present job or two years older in a new career? What are you waiting for?"

*Your talent determines what you can do.*
*Your motivation determines how much you are willing to do.*
*Your attitude determines how well you do it.*

~Lou Holtz

*Our finest moments are most likely to occur when we are feeling deeply uncomfortable, unhappy, or unfulfilled. For it is only in such moments, propelled by our discomfort, that we are likely to step out of our ruts and start searching for different ways or truer answers.*

~M. Scott Peck

# Contentment

*Contentment is not escape from the battle, but rather
an abiding peace and confidence in the midst of the battle.*

~Warren Wiersbe

F I ONLY HAD _____, I WOULD BE CONTENT. What's in the blank for you?

Is it to buy something, obtain this or that, or to achieve some promotion? When we get our desire, will we then be able to achieve happiness and secure peace of mind? It has been suggested that being content is a prerequisite for good mental health.

When I was a young boy, our family was considered poor. We did not, however, grow up deprived of life's basic needs of food, shelter, clothing...and fun. Contentment was not connected to possessions or lack thereof. For us, it was possible to have few possessions and be content. Yet, there are others who have more earthly goods and still remain discontented.

As a young boy, I was approached one day by a neighborhood parent who lived down the street and asked a question: "How can you be so happy...you have so little?" More surprised than offended, I did not have an answer. I certainly didn't see them as having anything I needed. Today I understand more fully the motive for their asking.

The material culture outside of our little neighborhood was creating that neighbor's discontentment. They had an internal battle of longing for more...better and bigger material prosperity. Their discontentment was created by comparing themselves to others who had more than they had. Socrates summed it up this way: "He who is not contented with what he has, would not be contented with what he would like to have."

As I grew older, my disposition didn't change. My attitude could be summed up by these words of Tom Gaskins: "To be content doesn't mean you don't desire more, it means you're thankful for what you have and patient for what's to come." Being at ease in one's body, mind, and situation are a choice and a perceptual state of mind. Living in the present, being grateful for today and hopeful for tomorrow, is an indication of much contentment and peace.

Don't misunderstand. There's nothing wrong with having goals or even noticing things that are desirable to have. Leaders are able to accept the reality of the present and trust the circumstances of life for its best. As leaders, we should avoid thinking in material and self-indulgent terms. Dwelling on the lifestyles of the rich and famous or wondering what it would be like to be someone else is not a healthy thought process.

I have witnessed the restless desires of others that drove their pursuits blindly forward. Their preoccupation with making and accumulating more observably impacted their character and leadership role in a negative way. There was an obvious discontent with the general quality of life. Some even acted with plans of stepping on others to get more for themselves. That "do whatever it takes" attitude of getting ahead does not go unnoticed by followers.

Our contentment doesn't mean neglecting or forgoing a better opportunity for a newer home, replacing a vehicle with a newer model, or planning for a more expensive vacation. Contentment also includes an accurate view of individual circumstances. It realizes the hard work required, the emotional disappointments to be dealt with realistically, and the ability to seize new opportunities when presented. It's this practical view of our individual circumstances that fulfills opportune moments in the future. In the process, contentment is also having a willingness and ability to postpone and not hold too tightly to the things we have or desire. Leadership has certainly taught us that nothing is permanent. A healthy attitude about contentment provides a greater long-term personal peace of mind.

*Remember, that which you now have was once among the things you hoped for.*

~Epicurus

*It is right to be contented with what we have,*
*But never with what we are.*

~JAMES MACKINTOSH

# Personal Profile

*Not for ourselves alone are we born.*

~Marcus Tullis Cicero

THE ULTIMATE JOB OF A LEADER IS TO SERVE. This service is the starting and ending point of all effective leadership.

Leaders desire to serve with credibility, a focus on core values, and by bringing passion and energy...just to name a few. But how are you wired? What drives you personally? What is your preferred "personal profile" for serving others? Since leaders cannot be autonomous, uniqueness and individuality are important qualities. And, by recognizing how we best serve, we are able to not only express it ourselves, but recognize it in others, and in doing so transfer the right assignments to the right people. It's also a guide to determining supervisory and management positions. This individual sensitivity to how we and others serve, when recognized by the leader, enhances the leader's ability to adjust specific tasks.

Our personal profile is also a means of identifying strengths and weaknesses, as well as understanding our desire for certain opportunities and tasks over others. It is also important to keep in mind that a personal profile can change with time and experience. As an example, take a moment and write your name with the opposite hand than you normally use. Was it awkward? Did it take more energy? Admit it: You could do it, but it wasn't your preference. Oftentimes, serving in ways inconsistent with a prolonged personal profile is like writing with our opposite hand.

It has been said that our personal profile can explain us, but it does not excuse us. Service to others is important. Mahatma Gandhi said it this way: "Those who focus on serving others to the best of their abilities live a life of greatness."

Complete the following exercise to get a better understanding of your personal profile to serving.

## How are you motivated?

1. I prefer to have lots of options and flexibility.
2. I prefer a plan and have order.

## How are you inspired?

1. I prefer to interact with a group.
2. I prefer to work alone or with one other person.

## How are you fulfilled?

1. I like others to show or explain to me what to do
2. I like to show and explain to others what to do.

*My three-number profile (one from each questioned section) is:*

\_\_\_\_\_ \_\_\_\_\_ \_\_\_\_\_

| | | |
|---|---|---|
| 1. *Unstructured* | Like a variety of activities, general guidelines, like to see progress and help where needed | |
| 2. *Structured* | Plan ahead, like order, detail oriented, focused, follow a schedule, see clearly | |
| 3. *Relational* | Accepted by others, guided by feelings, group "all in" relationships, the objective is to work with people | |
| 4. *Task* | Project oriented, ask "What's the goal?"; job needs to be completed, prefer limited interruptions, the objective is to complete tasks | |
| 5. *Asker* | Amiable, introvert, analytical | |
| 6. *Teller* | Expressive, emotional, assertive, control | |

*Know This*
Serving is for a lifetime.

*Consider This*
Consider a staff meeting to explain personal profile. Ask each staff member to complete one. Schedule a time to meet and discuss the results individually. Discuss with them any affirmation of their service or determine the willingness to overcome any fears of new challenges.

# Soft Skills

*Developing the right attitudes and attributes in people—such as*
*resilience, respect, enthusiasm, and creativity—is just*
*as important as academic or technical skills.*

~Neil Carberry

D O YOU PREFER SOMEONE WHO IS PERSONABLE, or
someone who treats you like a number in a long line of other num-
bers? As a leader who is influencing others, which "someone" do others
see you as being reflective of in their lives?

Hard skills, developed through education, training, and certifica-
tion, are job specific to demonstrating competence to complete assigned
tasks. Soft skills such as communication, creative thinking, and empathy lead to good habits and longer-term success. The soft skills of leaders
and followers alike represent those personal attributes, traits, and qualities that enable effective interaction with others. Soft skills are a leader's
social competences that allow for adaptability in times of change, and
ultimately define how you and I approach life and work.

A Stanford Research Institute survey of Fortune 500 companies
revealed that 75 percent of long-term job success was the result of personal soft skills. Soft skills, like hard skills, can be identified, learned,
and developed with practice and experience. Training that enhances
soft skills has a significant place in strengthening organizational policies and culture.

Where hard skills are quantitative and measurable through on-the-
job training, soft skills are measured in how well we handle relationships
with family, friends, coworkers, and customers in a variety of situations.
Soft skills are key to building relationships, gaining visibility, and creating opportunities for advancement. It has been said, "Technical skills

can get your foot in the door, but people skills are what opens future doors."

While soft skills can be job specific—like a human resources manager having the knack to give attention to detail, or a marketing consultant having good communications abilities—soft skills are not field restricted or job specific. Soft skills are transferable across all careers and industries. Soft skills can be noted through resumés, interviews, and promotional exams. You can be the best at what you do, but if your soft skills are lacking, you're limiting your chances for success.

### Soft Skills

| | | |
|---|---|---|
| Listening | Gives direction | Team player |
| Courteous | Competitive | Disciplined |
| Dependable | Multitask | Good attitude |
| Flexible | Loyal | Relational |
| Problem solver | Diligent | Positive influence |
| Communicator | Humble | Creative thinking |
| Respectful | Optimistic | Work ethic |
| Critical thinker | Eager to work | Completes tasks |
| Motivator | Desires to learn | Organized |
| Empathic | Confident | Integrity |
| Good humored | Follows instructions | Courageous |
| Resolves conflict | Confident | |

1. Select a soft skill you want to improve and practice it more consistently.

2. Find resources to help you look closer at that particular soft skill.

3. Observe and mimic the positive soft skill you see exhibited in others.

4. Set goals for improvement that include asking trusted friends for feedback.

Remember, soft skills are often undervalued, and training in them is seldom offered. As a leader, do not assume or expect followers to know how to treat people. Knowing how to build and maintain relationships is key. As Peggy Klaus noted, "Soft skills get little respect, but they will make or break your career." Soft skills are important to the success of all persons regardless of occupation. How are you doing with your soft skills?

# 87

# Resilient Leaders—Part I

*I can be changed by what happens to
me, but I refuse to be reduced by it.*

–Maya Angelou

DEATH, DIVORCE, ILLNESS, POVERTY, racism, and violence. Financial ruin, job loss, and public defamation. How do leaders deal with difficulties that impact, influence, and change lives? As author Eric Greitens points out, no one escapes pain, fear, and suffering. Yet from these come courage, wisdom, and strength. What is it then that enables us to adjust without being overcome? How do we develop and move forward within the highly responsible aspects of leadership? In part, the answer is...resilience. Resilience directly affects how we lead and influence others.

*Resilience* is an English word from the Latin for "springing back" or to "bounce back." Resilience has two distinct qualifiers: significant adversity and positive adaption. I have personally always viewed resilience as a "bouncing forward" from something or someplace, rather than just "getting back" to something or someplace. Psychology 101 tells us that resilience is "the ability to remain internally positive despite external negative influences in our lives." For me, resilience has always been the ability to envision a better future.

Resilience also has two components: cultural resilience and personal resilience. Cultural resilience is a focus on how a group identifies distinctively and maintains support through a common heritage, values, norms, virtues, and stories that help preserve us. Personal resilience is a focus on identifying those individual skills and strengths relied on to help us recover.

The Mayo Clinic has concluded that resilience is not the absence of pain, fear, grief, or anger. Resilience is the ability to function physically and psychologically by developing skills to become more resilient. Resilience isn't a single skill; it's a variety of coping mechanisms that resist giving up and letting heartbreak define us. The focus of the next three parts about resilient leaders will be on the components of personal resilience needed for those pivotal crossroad moments in life where negative experiences, decisions, and actions can serve to make us stronger.

*A 2017* Harvard Business Review *survey of 62 top executives revealed that 92 percent identified resilience as the most challenging aspect of leadership.*

### Resilience Check

Give yourself a number 1 to 10 rating on each of the statements below:

_____ I generally feel strong and capable of overcoming my problems.

_____ I generally stay calm when things get tough and stressful.

_____ I think well of myself and like who I am inside.

_____ Difficult times do not change the way I feel about myself.

_____ I enjoy life and am satisfied with my contribution within my sphere of influence.

_____ I am good at coping with strong negative emotions.

_____ I have goals, and I am optimistic about the future.

_____ I do not have self-destructive habits.

_____ I feel at peace with my past.

_____ My experiences have made me a stronger/better person.

_____ Total

No Resilience  0  10  20  30  40  50  60  70  80  90  100  Excellent Resilience

### Remember

Resilience is not the ability to escape unharmed or unaffected. There are scars to show for our life experiences.

*Disappointment is one thing. Defeatism is another.*

# 88

# Resilient Leaders—Part II

*Although the world is full of suffering, it is
full also of the overcoming of it.*

~HELEN KELLER

PHYSICAL, EMOTIONAL, AND SPIRITUAL RECOVERY lie in the hope that the personal challenges we experience are seen as opportunities for strengthening our personal resilience.

Psychologist and professor Norman Garmezy from the University of Minnesota was widely credited with the early study of the ability to overcome, succeed, and excel despite incredible difficulty. He identified this ability as resilience.

Later, psychologist and professor Emmy Warner from the University of California noted that resilience is basically a set of skills that can be taught and practiced in order to be strengthened at any age.

Master Resilience Training (MRT) is a comprehensive soldier initiative between the University of Pennsylvania and the United States Army base at Fort Leonard Wood, Missouri. Together they have identified three main areas for life skill development to address resilience training for soldiers and their families. The three areas are *mental toughness, strong relationships,* and *signature strengths.*

Let's consider *mental toughness.* Mental toughness is based on our thoughts and attitudes. At the core, it is a focus on developing an honest, positive understanding and reaction to events that affect us. This is accomplished by recognizing three distinct challenges. Number one: a staunch acceptance of reality. Ask yourself two basic questions: "What can I change?" and "What am I unable to change?" It takes initiative to think these through. Number two: accuracy in our thinking and understanding of the challenges we face. Primarily, that means realizing that asking for help is not a sign of weakness. And number three: understanding that the responsibility we have as leaders is not defined or changed by a role or title we hold. It's the attitude we have for leading ourselves and others that is our responsibility. These attitudes and thoughts represent our motivational nature realized in our acting and behaving the way we do.

### *Attitude is everything—pick a good one.*

The "Why?" question is not the most significant one. The most significant question we can ask ourselves is, "How do I respond?" Here are five key areas to consider in helping to develop and maintain mental toughness. Each results in a more positive direction for our leadership.

### Confidence:
Knowing what you stand for and those things you would not compromise on.

### Motivation:
Keeping in sight the bigger picture of what you have responsibility for.

### Accountability:
Trusting those closest to you to help you keep your standards, focus, and goals high.

### Positivity:
Choosing to elevate negative people and not bring yourself down with them.

### *A Word of Encouragement*

Resilience for leaders is always seeing an opportunity to grow and not give up.

The apostle Paul reassures us in Romans 5:3-5 that trouble brings perseverance; and perseverance, character; and proven character, hope; and hope does not disappoint.

# Resilient Leaders—Part III

*Resilience only comes from having been given the
chance to work through difficult problems.*

~GEVER TULLEY

STRONG RELATIONSHIPS IS THE SECOND component to resilient leadership. In addition to personal skills, this resource is needed to help enable our adaptability, problem solving, positive coping, and support. The care, respect, and trust that can come from strong relationships and meaningful interaction are critical and cannot be overlooked by the leader.

A 2017 *Harvard Business Review* survey of over 800 adults showed that 60 percent identified the biggest drain on their leadership was having to withstand criticism. Seventy-five percent identified with having to deal with difficult people. While constructive criticism is healthy, and difficult people are a challenge, it's those closest to you that represent your strongest relationships. If they have positive meaning to you, and you are willing to seek their assistance, you can push through all sorts of adversity.

Dr. Steven Wolin also reminds us that, in any culture, there are those that seek for us to adopt a victim mentality. Dwelling long term on burdens and vulnerabilities from any social, economic, environmental, or psychological cause can have a very negative effect. A very real caution is to be mindful of the conversations we have with ourselves. Our closest friends and associates help us identify with positive thoughts and ideas that can produce good personal action steps. Individual resilience then is inspired and defended by a focus on our greater reason and purpose for leading not only ourselves but others.

*Friends are those rare people who ask you how you*
*are doing and then wait to hear the answer.*

~Ed Cunningham

Without doubt, meaningful and positive communication, along with active listening—to ourselves as well as to others—is the key to any strong relationship. Dr. Edith Grothberg, PhD, suggests three basic personal thoughts to complete regarding building strong relationships: *I have—I am—I can.*

Are you able to answer with responses similar to these?

- *I have* taken responsibility for my life, identified role models, have respect for others, and have hope.

- *I am* a caring person, seeing my life as purposeful, a developing leader.

- *I can* seek good relationships, trust others, and become a better leader.

### The Key Dimension

The University of Michigan has recognized the need to identify with a "spiritual fitness" dimension to building resilience through personal relationships.

*The spiritual dimension is your center, your commitment to*
*your value system. It draws upon the sources that inspire and uplift you*
*and tie you to the timeless truths of humanity.*

~Steven Covey

Our spiritual dimension is that innermost self that provides us with a profound sense of who we are, where we came from, where we are going, and how we are going to get there.

May I suggest that the spiritual dimension we all need is God? His moral standard is the same for all people. We all fall short of His perfection. This is the reason our leadership and personal resilience require continual spiritual development.

God alone, through the redemptive work of Christ Jesus and the sustaining power of the Holy Spirit, is the One we need to be in relationship with to change any circumstance. It is a relationship that requires faith, repentance, forgiveness, and prayer.

# 90

# Resilient Leaders—Part IV

*Resilience takes place in the striving, not the accomplishing.*

~CHRISTIAN MOORE

"IT BUILDS CHARACTER" is a phrase we all have heard, especially growing up. It became a fill-in word for explaining hard work. *Signature strengths* is the third component of essential life skills for resiliency. Signature strengths are strongly held values and beliefs. They are identified through our personal character and applied to the effective behavior and specific results of the leader. Character determines what we choose to do with our experiences and relationships. Consistent behavior requires well-developed character traits to maintain personal resilience.

*Kharackter* is a Greek word meaning "an engraved mark or identification." Character is not a personality type like shy, outgoing, or smart. Personal resilience is about identifying, developing, and applying certain positive character qualities. These qualities are stable and distinct elements. They are a matter of conscience and an inward motivation to do right, and determine more consistent and effective behavior. Here are eight examples of key character traits of effective leaders desiring to be more resilient:

- Integrity
- Courage
- Discipline
- Loyalty
- Diligence
- Humility
- Optimism
- Conviction

Each character trait is a goal that helps you to become the type of leader others choose to respect and follow. Each trait is an expression of the genuine appreciation for the responsibilities a leader assumes. Each trait is a building block for a more resilient leader.

Do you desire to be a good leader? Effective leadership involves responsibility, experience, application, and a pursuit of the eight signature strengths.

*A pearl cannot be polished without friction,*
*nor a man perfected without trials.*

~CHINESE PROVERB

Here are six thought-provoking statements to consider in a pursuit of becoming a more resilient leader of character. Decide if you agree or disagree:

There is a difference between developing the appearance of leadership and the character of leadership.          Agree          Disagree

Personal character is always tested. Do not lose focus thinking once you have it, you cannot fail.          Agree          Disagree

In times of adversity, signature strengths (character) need to be balanced with other skills.          Agree          Disagree

There are times leaders awaken to the importance of character and are often overwhelmed with a sense of "I missed my moment."          Agree          Disagree

Character transcends all cultures because it deals with the daily struggle of human nature and adversity.          Agree          Disagree

### Closing Thought

Former Secretary of Education William Bennett's words about adversity summarize perfectly the importance of encouraging more resilient leaders:

In times like these you may need every virtue in your arsenal to help you stand fast...perseverance, courage, self-discipline, responsibility, integrity. And, you may need the loyalty of friendship of one or two good companions, as well as faith in God to see you through the struggle.

*The more we are exposed to what constitutes effective leadership, the more likely we internalize the same values and behaviors.*

~POINTMAN LEADERSHIP INSTITUTE

# 91

# Honoring Age and Experience

*We get old too soon and wise too late.*

~BENJAMIN FRANKLIN

I N ANCIENT ROME, THE ELDERLY were shown high regard. Their advice was welcomed, and much faith was placed in the counsel they had to offer. This was a way of acknowledging that wisdom can be accrued through years and experience. Marcus Cicero, a Roman statesmen, was considered one of Rome's greatest orators. Cicero noted, "There is assuredly nothing dearer to a man than wisdom, and though age takes all else, it undoubtedly brings us that." Oscar Wilde stated, "Experience is simply the name we give our mistakes." Vern Law described experience with these words: "Experience is a hard teacher because she gives the test first and the lesson afterwards."

Common decency would seem to indicate that we would honor our elders with dignity, appreciation, and admiration. We should recognize the weightiness and substantiality of their years of experience. Sadly, this sentiment grows increasingly forgotten in much of society. We often neglect those with debilitating conditions by our attitudes and practices. What is your attitude toward those who have gone before you?

With our parents, teachers, and first employers, we learn what it is like to have someone older and more experienced in authority over us. Sometimes it was a challenge to listen to them, honor them, and do the things we didn't want to, as we sought our independence. And while not every person is worthy of 100 percent of our love and affection, we do need to find ways to show gratefulness for what we have received from others. Our gratitude should be found in the positive things.

Failing to recognize and show this honor is equal to outright disrespect. It's often the result of being taken captive by bitterness (as with parents) or by envy (as with employers). While leadership positions can be abused, we should strive to overcome the pain, rejection, and emptiness caused by those who have at a minimum given us our very life. So, even in the absence of a great father, we can seek to be a better father. In the absence of a great boss or leader, we can seek to be a better boss and leader. As Helen Keller pointed out, "Only through trial and suffering can the soul be strengthened, ambition inspired, and success achieved." We should strive to not let destructive thoughts and attitudes control our own development of good character and our ability to recognize how others have contributed to our lives.

Honoring age and experience is simply acknowledging those making significant contributions to our lives. Regardless of our circumstances, and whatever has happened in the past, we need to identify those who have contributed to who we are through the impact of their own lives. Those who have given us a chance by hiring us, teaching us, and correcting us, all while supporting us. They have shared their own life lessons of enduring adversity, overcoming trials, and dealing with change. In doing so, we also begin to demonstrate for those following behind us how to transition well through the experiences and aging of life we all must face.

*Aging is not lost youth, but a new stage of opportunity and strength.*

~BETTY FRIEDAN

### Honoring Age and Experience

Spend time with them. Listen to their stories. Ask for advice. Discuss family heritage. Send a letter or card. Make a personal phone call. Tell others close to them how much you have appreciated them. It will get back to them. Remember to not make age a determining factor in choosing relationships.

# Balance

*Unless a person takes charge of them, both*
*work and free time are likely to be disappointing.*

–Mihgly Csikszentmihalyi

I CAN'T KEEP DOING THIS." As a leader, have you ever found yourself thinking that thought? It's a personal reflection and frustration that something has to change but is difficult to do. In a position of leadership, you might feel the overwhelming need to press the limit of your physical, mental, and emotional strength to succeed. While such commitment can certainly be noticed, it may be that a more deliberate look at life is needed in order to achieve greater personal balance.

Bill Walton, the cofounder of Holiday Inns, shared his story. He helped build a great corporation. But to do so, he arrived at the office every morning before seven and rarely got home before ten o'clock at night. He then added that he never saw a single Little League baseball game. I believe Mr. Walton shared that personal story of disappointment to help offer perspective and to encourage others to reorder their priorities.

When you hit a pothole in the road, it sometimes knocks your wheel out of balance, and your car begins to wobble down the road. If you don't take your car in to the tire shop to get it fixed, it could cause a dangerous accident later on. The same is true of your life. The busyness of life, along with pressure to succeed and get ahead, can cause life to become wobbly and out of balance.

When that happens, we need to slow down and determine what has caused the imbalance and how to reestablish priorities. A balanced life requires purposely looking at other important aspects needing attention. It means not pushing on after it's clear that a more stable environment of work, activity, and rest is evident. Let me share with you something I refer to as the "Stewardship of Life."

A three-legged stool requires balance. Each leg of the stool represents time invested with others. Let's label the legs of the stool *Family*, *Work*, and *Social*. If any one of the legs is weakened, neglected, or shortened, the overall balance and stability of the care for personal health and life is affected.

*Family* represents our physical well-being, closest relationships, health, and security. It can also represent time to read, write, or enjoy a hobby.

*Work* represents our intellectual well-being and ability to earn a living and save. This can include conferences, mentors, and learning new skills.

*Social* represents our extended community and well-being. It indicates our need for social fellowship and relationships. For some, that points to church and spiritual growth in relationship to God and with others in all areas of life.

Is your stool wobbly or out of balance at this time? It might be good to strengthen one of the legs before collapse occurs and you end up in a heap on the floor—or in the hospital.

Which legs do you feel might need more stabilization or balance? Are some areas more important than others? Are you missing any Little League games?

> *Balance happens when I invite it to happen with my*
> *intentional actions and my guided perspective.*
>
> ~MARY ANNE RADMACHER

# Questions

*I never learn anything talking.*
*I only learn things when I ask questions.*

~LOU HOLTZ

**W**HY DO WE ASK QUESTIONS? The answer is quite simple. We're curious about some topic, and a question provides a unique doorway to answers and knowledge. Who then asks the most questions? One survey suggested it was four-year-old girls, who averaged 390 questions a day.

Albert Einstein once said, "If I had an hour to solve a problem and my life depended on the solution, I would spend the first 55 minutes determining the proper question to ask for once I know the proper question, I could solve the problem in less than five minutes." Questions help us to:

- Learn
- Build relationships
- Counsel others
- Avoid misunderstanding

- Defuse conflict
- Persuade thinking in others
- Gain wisdom
- Satisfy curiosity

There are different types of questions that help us to gain insight, provide knowledge, and satisfy our curiosity.

   ✓ **Closed Questions**—generate one-word or short
     answers:
    *"Did you close the window?"*
    *"Is it cold outside?"*

✓ **Open-ended Questions**—elicit longer answers. These questions often begin with words like *who, what, when, why,* or *how:*
*"Why do you think the meeting was a failure?"*
*"How do you plan to accomplish your goal?"*

✓ **Funnel Questions**—often start with a closed question followed by a series of general questions that get more specific as they drill down:
*"How many people were at the conference?"*
*"Which companies were represented?"*
*"Who were some of the speakers?"*
*"How did one speaker stand out from the others?"*
*"What did they say that challenged you personally?"*

✓ **Probing Questions**—help to give you insight, gain information, and clarify responsibility and accountability:
*"Exactly what statistics do you want in the report?"*
*"When do you want the project completed and who is going to be responsible for sharing the decision with the accounting department?"*

✓ **Leading Questions**—move the listener toward the questioner's point of view or way of thinking:
*"Don't you think Grace made an outstanding presentation today?"*
*"Between the decision to buy the property or simply rent it, don't you think it makes more sense to buy and own the property outright?"*

✓ **Rhetorical Questions**—aren't really questions as much as they are statements. They can also take on a form of leading the listener's thinking:
*"This is the best apple pie in the world, don't you think?"*
*"Isn't that the greatest advertising presentation you've ever seen?"*

*"Don't you like the way they put the talking cow in the living room?"*

## The Three Most Important Questions in Counseling Others

1. What's going on?...*"What's on your mind?"*
2. How do you feel about it?...*"What do you want?"*
3. Do you want to change?...*"What's the biggest challenge for you?"*

*If I had to do it again, I'd ask more questions
and interrupt fewer answers.*

~ROBERT BRAULT

# Followership

*He who cannot be a good follower, cannot be a good leader.*

~ARISTOTLE

"LEAD, FOLLOW, OR GET OUT OF THE WAY." While attributed to General George S. Patton, the quote is not intended to be a statement about bravado or a constant drive at all costs. The general's actual quote reads like this; "We herd sheep, we drive cattle, we lead people. Lead me, follow me, or get out of my way." It's more reasonable to see this as a respectful request for being actively led, actively followed, or actively stepping aside from being a hindrance to the goal.

Let's take a brief look at a few myths about followership:

- *Followership is the opposite of leadership.* False: Both are significantly complementary to the same purpose.

- *Followership is blind obedience.* False: One should never concede to doing something immoral, unethical, or illegal.

- *Followership is disingenuous.* False: To be liked over the risk of being truthful is always harmful.

- *Followership doesn't require training.* False: Certain practical skills are always required, but character development and application are pivotal to both.

A follower has been described as someone who ascribes to the teaching and methods of another. A leader has been described as someone inspiring others to a common purpose and goal. While leaders are viewed as having direct control and influence, followers are also extended this control and influence within their spheres of responsibility. This is often overlooked. Have you ever attended a seminar and heard someone say, "I wish my boss could hear this"? Both leadership and followership require dedicated people to serve where they are. They are representatives and ambassadors of a higher authority. And many of the same qualities admired in leaders are the same qualities appreciated in followers: dedication, service, work ethic, and self-motivation.

*Leaders establish policy...Followers conduct themselves within policy.*
*Leaders concentrate on effectiveness...Followers ensure readiness.*
*Leaders set the standards...Followers embrace the standards.*
*I lead, therefore I follow.*

~Pointman Leadership Institute

Regardless of the title or position, the need to juggle both roles is essential. How is that accomplished? Take a look at the questions below. They are helpful in realizing the transition between the roles of leader and follower.

- Are you accepting of goals and committed to delivering on what is expected?

- Do you develop areas of personal strength to complement the authority over you?

- Do you accept the position and work preferences of those who are in charge?

- Do you champion the need for changes, and are you giving input for improvements?

- Do you take appropriate action in the absence of any direct responsibility over you?

- Do you have a team view of the organization and take directions from others?

- Are you willing to set the example for those observing you from all directions?

- Can you trust your future to and achieve your goals through those in control?

### Something to Think About

Conductor Leonard Bernstein reflected that "the most difficult instrument to play in the orchestra is the second fiddle." He went on to mention that's true of all second instruments. He concluded by saying, "If no one plays second, there is no harmony."

Followers take responsibility for the quality of leadership. Leaders take responsibility for the quality of followers. They endorse each other.

*Keep in mind that followership, like leadership, is a role and responsibility, not a stepping-stone to a destination.*

# A Volunteering Leader

*The best way to find yourself is to lose yourself in the service to others.*

~Mahatma Gandhi

ALL THAT WE SEND INTO THE LIVES OF OTHERS comes back into our own" is a line from the "Creed Poem" by Edwin Markham. Markham was an American poet. His words speak to the truth of the purpose we have toward the lives of other human beings. And in the process of fulfilling that truth, we actually discover we have become a stronger person ourselves.

Whether volunteering through a specific service project such as a soup kitchen, food pantry, animal shelter, providing an educational opportunity through speaking on character, demonstrating how to cook a meal, or teaching CPR, it has been proven that volunteering changes lives. Within a local community or by traveling a greater distance, there are invaluable opportunities to enhance the lives of others and experience something special for ourselves. How often have we heard from someone returning from a mission trip opportunity? They recount the experience with feelings of having received more of a personal benefit and blessing than those they actually went to serve.

Authors Leith Anderson and Jill Fox point out that in a national survey of 3,351 adults, 76 percent of those who volunteered say that doing so made them feel healthier. In a separate study, the London School of Economics agreed and reported significant health stability in those who volunteer. Seventy-eight percent indicated that volunteering lowered stress. And 94 percent said that volunteering improved their overall mood and outlook on life. They also pointed out that those who volunteer as a group solve problems more quickly. It was also noted there was an increase in job retention of those who volunteer. In short, volunteering is the difference between being a successful leader or being a significant leader.

*No man can sincerely help another without helping himself.*

~Ralph Waldo Emerson

*Consider the following list of service ideas for ways to give back to others, as well as for a way to reflect on the potential values of volunteering for you, your family, or your staff:*

### Service Ideas

Donate clothes to a shelter

Assemble care packages for soldiers

Read books at a children's hospital

Teach a lesson on budgeting

Present tips on child safety

Help serve a meal at a shelter

Do random acts of kindness

Teach a texting class to seniors

Share on preparing a simple budget

Present tips on child safety

### Realized Values

Opportunity to learn from others

Improve communication skills

Move out of comfort zones

Support of emotional well-being

Key to a more positive attitude

Build one's self-esteem

Strengthen character/aptitudes

Gain more personal independence

Experience new tasks/new people

Help the process of aging gracefully

If you want your leadership, family, or organization to grow—volunteer. If you want your leadership, family, and organization to impact others—volunteer. The question is, Will you seize the initiative? Being a volunteer provides one of the most rewarding experiences imaginable. Being able to share those experiences with others makes a lifetime of memories.

### Interesting to Note

There is no anticipated social or financial gain to be expected from volunteering. However, the Independent Sector, an organization that gathers statistics on volunteerism, places an estimated worth of a volunteer's time to the group being served at a value of $25.43 an hour.

Check with local churches, schools, and community groups. Think skills, interests, values, and availability. Take time to volunteer for a greater opportunity to help balance work and life.

# 96

# Who's Following?

*Leaders don't force people to follow; they invite them on a journey.*

"N O ORGANIZATION CAN DO BETTER THAN the people it has." Peter Drucker was pointing out that while people determine the performance capacity of an organization, leaders are only as strong as the people who come along to support them and the mission. As vital as followership is to both the leader and the organization, not much is said about developing followers.

Aubrey Malphurs points out that the leader can identify the level of followership in a number of specific ways:

1. Followers can be those who sense an immediate need to be led in the organization's mission.

2. Followers can be those who sense a need to be led and are willing to follow, but need time to experience the trustworthiness of the leader.

3. Followers can be those who have been part of past leadership failures and do not want to risk the strain and pain again.

4. Followers can be those who have been so influenced by a particular leader that they do not want to see the next leader succeed.

5. Followers can be those who will never commit to follow because of a rebellious spirit.

A true follower is one who is both able and willing to get behind legitimate leadership to accomplish goals. They might even oppose or challenge that leadership from time to time for the right reasons. You might want to ask yourself some questions about the people who follow your leadership:

- Do they know where the organization is headed?
- Do they want to go where the organization is headed?
- Do they believe that your leadership team is competent to take them there?
- Do they have the necessary knowledge and experience to follow?
- Do they have the maturity and self-esteem to be a significant follower?

It's a leader's responsibility to help their followers develop their potential and grow in their skills. You can't force growth, but you can encourage it with positive leadership behaviors. As a leader, you also need to be aware of negative behaviors that discourage those under your leadership.

*The growth and development of people*
*is the highest calling of leadership.*

**~Harvey Firestone**

| Positive Behaviors | Negative Behaviors |
|---|---|
| Recognition | Micromanagement |
| Clear directions | Workaholic expectations |
| Your time | Unreasonable pressure |
| Develop potential | Isolation |
| Learning opportunities | Self-evaluations |
| Harmless joking | Lack of communications |
| Light competition | Questionable job security |
| Saying "well done" | No follow-through |
| Annual reviews | Unexplained changes |
| Personal notes | Only negative feedback |
| Defined roles | Disparaging comments |

### *Food for Thought*

One day the lion decided to be sure all the other animals knew he was king. He went to each one and asked, "Who is the king of this jungle?" They all replied, "It's you, Mr. Lion." At last he came alone to the elephant and posed the same question. The elephant grabbed the lion with his trunk, whirled him around, thrust him into the water, then slammed him to the ground. The lion—beaten, bruised, and shocked—looked at the elephant and proclaimed, "Just because you don't know the answer is no reason to get upset."

*You can proclaim, "I'm the leader, I'm the leader,"*
*but if you have no followers, you are only out for a walk.*

# 97

# Strengthening Families

*Family may not be the best experience,*
*but it is always the most important.*

~WINSTON CHURCHILL

THE GRANDPARENTS WERE CELEBRATING their golden wedding anniversary. The grandmother told the secret of their long and happy marriage: "On my wedding day, I decided to make a list of ten of my husband's faults...which for the sake of our marriage I would over-look." A granddaughter quickly asked, "Grandma, what were the ten faults?" The grandmother replied, "Oh, I never did get around to making the list. But whenever your grandfather did something that made me mad, I would say to myself, 'Lucky for him that's one of the ten.'"

Marriage and family are two of the oldest institutions designed for the good of humanity. Society thrives on strong families. Family is the place in which people tend to find both the greatest meaning and fulfillment, as well as profound frustration and pain. There are always things to disagree about, but family should be the first and the last safe place we know. Marriage and families are simply unique unions of personalities, opinions, and shortcomings.

The success of marriages and families should be the greatest of all leadership pursuits. While no family or marriage is perfect, they continue to represent one of the oldest and most resilient institutions illustrating the security, dependability, and confidence that all followers seek from leaders. As Winston Churchill pointed out, "There is no doubt that it is around the family and the home that all the greatest virtues are created, strengthened, and maintained."

Look at this survey list of the top ten reasons and statistical percentages given for the breakdown of marriages and families:

- Lack of commitment—75%
- Infidelity—59.6%
- Arguing/conflict—57.7%
- Married too young—45.1%
- Financial problems—36.1%

- Substance abuse 34.6%
- Domestic violence—23.5%
- Health issues—18.2 %
- Lack of support—17.3 %
- Religious differences—13.3%

Like the story of the grandmother, it is not always easy to dismiss our feelings for the intended purpose of strengthening relationships. It takes a deep level of intentionality to demonstrate the small sacrifices needed and the dedication required for building strong family relationships. Consider this list of intentional actions to strengthening marriages and families.

Compliment them regularly in both private and with others.

Connect with your spouse and family members on a daily basis.

Take care of your appearance, and make plans to do things together.

Give opportunities to spend time apart with friends and to enjoy a hobby.

Give small gifts occasionally just as a way of showing you're thinking about them.

Say "I love you" every day in person, with phone calls, and through text messaging.

Review often together the growth and progress you see in your marriage and family.

*And when difficulties come, be sure to say,*
*"I'm sorry...Please forgive me...Can we start again?"*

Strong marriages and families are directly related to the leader's influence and followership of others. If a leader's marriage and family—regarded as the most valuable of societal relationships—are neglected, dishonored, and violated by the leader, won't the followers believe that they will be neglected, dishonored, and violated also?

*The strength of family, like the strength of an army,
is in its loyalty to each other.*

~MARIO PUZO

# 98

# Actions, Behavior, Conduct

*A good man out of the good treasure of his heart brings forth good;*
*and an evil man out of the evil treasure of his heart brings forth*
*evil. For out of the abundance of the heart his mouth speaks.*

~Luke 6:45 nkjv

JOHN LOCKE, ONE OF OUR EARLY AMERICAN founders said, "I have always thought the actions of men the best interpreters of their thoughts."

It's interesting that when we look at our own actions, behavior, and conduct, we judge ourselves by our impulses, desires, ideas, reasons, motives, or intentions. But when we look at the behavior of others, we judge them by their actions and conduct, not their motives or intentions.

Why do we do that? It's because we really have no idea what their intentions are. We only see their actions, not their motives.

You see, in life the bottom line is that people do what they want to do. Often their intentions are good in their own mind. They see no wrong in what they are doing and have plenty of personal reasons and excuses for their behavior. But sometimes their actions and behavior cause or create conflict with others. That probably gave rise to the comment that says, "The road to hell is paved with good intentions."

Matthew Good said, "Actions speak louder than words. And sometimes inaction speaks louder than both of them." Patrick Ness comments, "You do not write your life with words...You write it with actions. What you think is not important. It is only important what you do."

For example, you don't want to fall in love with someone who says the right things. You want to fall in love with someone who does the right things. Talk is okay, but it must be backed up by action. It's important that they show you by conduct every little way possible that they want you. Talk is easy and cheap. Where's the effort?

Let's say I owe you some money, which you need paid back by a certain date. I told you, "You can count on me. You'll have your money by then." What happens when I miss paying you back? How do you feel? What do you think about me? Not too good, I bet.

In my mind I simply got busy and forgot about it, or some event occurred in my life. Maybe my car broke down, and I needed to pay the bill. I had full intention to pay you back, but didn't. In my mind, I have a ton of excuses for my failure to keep my word. I even feel sorrowful about it. Spurgeon, the great preacher, said, "Sorrow pays no debt."

Back to the comment that people do in life what they want to do. Everyone's behavior has to do with choices. Johann Wolfgang von Goethe suggested, "Behavior is the mirror in which everyone shows their image."

*"What you are speaks so loudly that I can't hear what you are saying."* When you look into the mirror of your life, what do you see? Are you a person of integrity? Do your words match your deeds? Have you made promises or commitments that you have not honored with your spouse, your children, those you work with, your church? Actions prove who someone is; words prove who they "wanna" be.

This is not a day to make excuses and justifications or to fall back on intentions. Benjamin Franklin said, "Well done is better than well said." This next week is a time for action and behavior change.

### *Just Do It!*

*But let each one examine his own work...*
*Do not be deceived, God is not mocked;*
*for whatever a man sows, that he will also reap.*

~Galatians 6:4-7

# Finishing Well

*It is the spirit that motivates, that calls upon our resources of
dedication and effort, that decides whether we will give our best,
finish strong, or just do enough to get by.*

~PETER DRUCKER

O PEN YOUR EYES, LOOK WITHIN. Are you satisfied with the
life you're living?" A very challenging question from Bob Marley,
don't you think? The idea of finishing well has both a tangible and intan-
gible result. As a leader, you can look back at a list of responsibilities and
accomplishments and feel a certain level of achievement. As a leader, we
can realize personal satisfaction for having made intelligent and timely
decisions affecting morale. But, if we're being honest, the temptation
to avoid a realistic view of finishing well may result in mediocre service.
In that sense, finishing well could equate only to pursuing success, and
neglect the important factor of significance. Both are honorable and
require our time, sacrifice, and energy.

Success has a primary focus on personal plans, goals, and objectives.
Its purpose is the attainment of earnings and recognition through education, opportunities, experience, and vocational achievement. All are
important. However, success can be carried out with an ego that com-
promises values, is motivated by selfishness, and is sought by what others can do for us.

Significance, on the other hand, is driven by a conviction to personal
principles, character, and a desired set of behaviors that focus on adding
meaning and importance to others. Objectives and goals become less
about you and me and more about influencing and impacting others.

The key to retaining a healthy view of success and significance, with
the ability to finish well, is our depth of perspective regarding those future

generations we are responsible for influencing. The questions we must all ask ourselves are these: "Do I realize my purpose in life?" "Who is deciding what 'finishing well' means?" "Do I want to be successful or significant?"

*Success is what happens to you.*
*Significance is what happens through you.*

~Keith Craft

Jack and Gary Kinder have identified some characteristics of leaders who desire to move from success to significance. Do these describe you?

1. Leaders think highly of their work endeavor and make reasonable commitments.

2. Leaders respond to responsibilities and enjoy improving things.

3. Leaders are realistic, practical, and bounce back from discouragement.

Truett Cathy, founder of Chick-fil-A restaurants, provides these additional qualities:

- Do not be burdened with personal debt. Sacrifice material things and reward yourself later.

- Observe what is working in the lives of others (character). Do not try to please all people.

- Set priorities in their proper order. Be prepared for disappointments and failure.

- Invite God to be involved in every decision, and honor God with your abilities.

Dr. George Crane of Northwest University emphasized a spiritual component to being a significant leader that he described as a personal inner strength and optimism.

*Our lives matter so much to God...*
*He wants us involved in His eternal purposes.*

~Dr. Gerry Lewis

The ability to finish well is not found in the capacity to impress others, but rather in a commitment to the right endeavors. Is your desire to be useful and responsible? Do you have a deep passion and belief in knowing that what is being fulfilled is of greater service? Can you and I remain true to the mission, have a positive influence on others, and be a faithful steward of all that has been entrusted to us? Yes, we can. Finishing well is measured by realizing that God gives the opportunities and the ability to fulfill the responsibilities we have been given. With success, we become a product of our good work. With significance, we become a product of God's greater work. Which one do you desire to identify with more?

# Six Pieces of Paper

*The two most important days in your life are the day
you are born and the day you find out why.*

–Mark Twain

SEVERAL YEARS AGO, I ATTENDED A MEETING where the
speaker handed out paper and asked us to tear it into six equal pieces.
He then asked us to write down on each piece of paper the six most
important things in life to us—one item on each piece of paper.

He mentioned that we might consider things like our health, our
spouse, our children, our career, our friendships, our pets, and a number of other items. He then asked us to pick up those pieces of paper and
hold them in one hand. He told us to fan them out so that we could see
them—similar to holding six cards in your hand.

Next, he talked about how tragedy comes into the life of everyone.
He mentioned that we can lose our job, we can lose our health, and we
can lose our loved ones through death. Everything was going fine until
he said, "We are going to imagine that tragedy is going to strike your
life today. You will have to give up one of the six things in your hand—
never to have it ever again. Pull out one of the pieces of paper and place
it on the table in front of you."

Everyone groaned at the decision they had to make. Then he talked a
little more about tragedy and told us that it had just struck a second time.
We would have to place another one of the six most important things in
our life on the table. More groans and rumblings could be heard through
the audience as they gave up a second item—never ever to have it again.

This exercise in priorities continued until we only had one piece of
paper in our hands. He said, "I want you to look at the piece of paper left
in your hand. If you have anything written on it like an item of value or

a person that you love, I want you to be aware that tragedy could strike and take that important thing from you. Then, where would you be? If, however, you have written something like God or a relationship with God—that can never be taken from you."

That turned out to be a very sobering evaluation of what was truly important to us. In turn, I might ask you the same question. If you went through the same exercise, what would be the most important thing in your life? Would it be things that could perish? Would it be a relationship with a loved one that could be lost? Or would you write down "a relationship with God"?

When it comes to spiritual matters, there seem to be three general categories of people. With which category would you identify yourself?

1. The "Whatevers." There are those who could not care less about spiritual matters. They do not have any background in religious faith and do not feel a need to develop one. Or if they do have some previous knowledge, they have chosen to reject it for various reasons.

2. The "Ah-ahs!" These are those who may or may not have some spiritual background but are interested in the topic. They are seekers who are open to consider this avenue of life and would like further information.

3. The Thinkers. These are those who are deeply concerned about spiritual matters. Their emotional and mental health are tied closely to their faith and how it affects their daily life. They strive in various degrees to attempt to grow in their faith and knowledge.

Those who are interested or are deeply concerned about spiritual matters identify with the words of Jesus when He says, "For what profit is it to a man if he gains the whole world, and loses his own soul? Or what will a man give in exchange for his soul?" (Matthew 16:26 NKJV).

### What would you write on your last piece of paper?

*For God so loved the world that He gave*
*His only begotten Son, that whoever believes in Him*
*should not perish but have everlasting life.*

~John 3:16 NKJV

# Potholes

*God can help you to endure the large potholes
in the journey of life.*

LIFE IS NOT ALWAYS AN EASY ROAD. Sometimes we encounter the "potholes" of difficulties, the bypasses of anxiety, the pain of bumps, and the detours of depression. During these times of uncomfortableness, it's easy to become weary of it all. Are you tired and weary of the pressures in your life and the various troubles you face? Then join the club. Many people feel the same way.

The Bible suggests that God does care about you and the problems you face. God wants to come to your aid and help you through the tough times—the times that cause anxiety and depression.

Jesus said, "Come to Me, all you who labor and are heavy laden, and I will give you rest. Take My yoke upon you and learn from Me, for I am gentle and lowly in heart, and you will find rest for your souls. For My yoke is easy and My burden is light" (Matthew 11:28-30 NKJV).

How does someone come to Jesus? How does a person find rest for their soul? How can I experience peace—overcoming anxiety and depression—in the midst of turmoil? Jesus said, "Peace I leave with you, My peace I give to you; not as the world gives do I give to you. Let not your heart be troubled, neither let it be afraid" (John 14:27 NKJV).

The apostle Paul states it this way:

> *That if you confess with your mouth the Lord Jesus and believe in your heart that God has raised Him from the dead, you will be saved. For with the heart one believes unto righteousness, and with the mouth confession is made unto salvation...For "whoever calls on the name of the LORD shall be saved."*
>
> ~Romans 10:9-10,13 NKJV

Have you ever done that before? If not, you can do it right now. Just put down this book and pray a simple prayer of faith asking Jesus to come into your life. Thank Him for dying in your place. Thank Him for providing a new relationship with God. Ask God to bring people into your life who can help you to grow and learn more about Him. Thank Him for saving you.

Do you remember as a small child flying a kite? You would run with the kite held high until the wind caught it and it began to soar into the sky. If you had a long string, the kite would rise higher and higher. Eventually, the kite would be so high that it would seem to disappear. The way that you could tell that the kite was still there was by the tug on the string caused by the wind. In the same way, God gives a tug on the strings of our heart. Something inside of you senses that God is calling you to make a decision for Christ. You may feel like I am talking to you personally. If you have that feeling, it's the tug of God. It's certainly not my writing that's stirring your soul. I'm only a messenger bringing you "good news."

When someone invites Jesus to come into his or her life, God sends His Holy Spirit to dwell within. He will be there to teach you about God. He will support you in tough times. He will help you to endure the pain and suffering that have been ravaging you because of anxiety and depression. He will teach you how to overcome these negative feelings.

# Quick Tips to Becoming a Leader You'd Want to Follow

You know a strong leader when you see one, but Bob Phillips is here to show you how to step into that person's shoes. After directing a multimillion-dollar organization and heading leadership seminars worldwide, he knows exactly what makes a leader great and what you need to do to more effectively guide others.

With over 50 thoughtful and concise chapters you can read in ten minutes or less, Bob will prepare you to be a more dynamic and compassionate leader. With biblical wisdom, engaging illustrations, and motivational thoughts from world-renowned leaders from all fields, you will...

- uncover the qualities and habits you need to sharpen your abilities
- identify how you can best handle the struggles that come with authority
- fill your toolbox with skills and strategies taken from those with more experience

Whether you're at the beginning of your journey or nearing the summit, *Leadership Success in Ten Minutes a Day* is a straightforward, outcome-oriented resource that will give you the direction and encouragement you need to succeed.